Trigger On!

I0117964

Brandon D Freeman

chipmunkapublishing

the mental health publisher

Published by

Chipmunkapublishing

PO Box 6872

Brentwood

Essex CM13 1ZT

United Kingdom

http://www.chipmunkapublishing.com

Edited by Jennifer Freeman

ISBN   978-1-84991-664-6

Chipmunkapublishing gratefully acknowledge the support of Arts Council England.

Trigger On!

This book is dedicated to my wife and children without them it would have been impossible to recover from this debilitating illness.

Brandon D Freeman

Prelude

I remember running through the woods on my grandpa's farm in the Ozarks. Sometimes he would let us take an old 22 with us and try to scare up some turkeys, or maybe a squirrel or two. Of course, we would never hit anything. Another time when I was thirteen, my father, uncles, and grandpas all decided to take a hunting trip in Marysville, Kansas on my grandma's farm. I finally was old enough to go along. I had an old single shot twenty gauge Winchester. You know the kind-You had to load it from the back and when you popped it open, the gun smoke poured out of it after every shot. That kind. I used to love that part of the engagements with the pheasant and quail. I didn't care what I hit; I just liked to watch the shell fly out the back when I popped it open. The smell of gunpowder and seeing what I hit all dead and bloody made me proud that I accomplished something when I hunted. I looked forward to the days when I could take my own sons out and teach them how to shoot and hunt the way my father and grandfather taught me. I still have a picture somewhere of all the men in the family standing behind a big truck with all the kills they made that day of pheasant and quail.

Now I have pictures in my mind of dead people. Amazing how that works, isn't it. From one innocent childhood memory of happiness, I am how haunted by pictures of war and violence. I fast forwarded to the Gulf War and hunting again. I was nineteen and just got back from the Gulf in 1991. With my fiancée Jennifer by my side we went with my family back up to grandma's farm and I took the old 20 gauge my father gave me when I was a kid. My grandma wanted me to go shoot the squirrels that were tearing apart her barn and eating her garden. Two things happened that day which I will never forget. First my mother being overprotective as she was, and clueless as ever, told me before I went out that I would have to take my father with me before I hunted. I thought, that was unbelievable. I had just returned from war, and she wanted my dad to go with me to hunt pesky squirrels. The second thing came to me as quite the surprise.

I was walking toward the creek were I usually found something to shoot when I was a kid, and there they were, two big squirrels. The squirrels were munching on the corner of my grandma's barn. I clicked the shotgun open and loaded a round. I could probably get both of them if I aimed just right. I lowered the sight on both of them, put pressure on the trigger, and then I stopped. Watching them munch on the barn. I lifted the gun again and put pressure on the trigger again. Then I stopped again. For some reason shooting them wasn't the same as before. In anger and hatred for that ridiculous emotion I was feeling at the time. I pointed the gun at the trash barrel near them and pulled the trigger. The loud blast scared off the two mischievous squirrels. Plus, I wanted everyone in the house to think I was doing my job clearing away grandma's squirrel problem.

That very second in time, I knew I had a problem. A rifle range at work was fine. Practicing to kill things was fine. We did it in the Gulf war. Heck sometimes in the Gulf we killed each other. It is the nature of the beast; however, I realized that I didn't like the feeling of killing anymore. That I had a real problem with doing it. Doing that to people or things changes people and it changed me. Little did I know that I would be leading men in Baghdad almost fourteen years later.

Our main patrol area in Baghdad was Abu-Graib, however, our unit served in Sadr-City as well. My platoon, in particular, served and did all our patrols in Abu-Graib. This is where all my nightmares come from. I was having a serious loss of sleep, changing of moods, a whole lot of emotional up and down swings, and a loss of sexual activities with my wife when I returned from the war. Classic signs of PTSD.

For years I found comfort in internet sex after I returned this didn't' stop once I was a drill instructor for the Army. That eventually would be my downfall. I was charged with showing my genitals to a lower enlisted soldier over the internet from my cell phone. The only problem with this charge is at that time I was having major flash backs. I was out of control. I needed help, attempted to get help, and was denied. My last effort finally ended with me in mental health facilities for the next sixty days. When you get that low, the only way out is an unquestionable act.

The circle of guilt- that I call anger, depression, bargaining, and acceptance -filled my waking hours. I couldn't break free. This story is how I felt in my darkest hours and how I felt on a daily basis in the mental hospitals. You are about to enter my darkness.

Warning, what you are about to read may trigger flash backs. Take your time reading this. There is no hurry. Remember; to understand makes you powerful; knowledge and communication are essential. So relax you can do this.

Trigger On!

Part One

"The Darkness has Fallen"

DAY 2, 28SEPT2007

> The pain never ends! Stop the pain!! Get out of my head!! Suck it up, grunt! A soldier never quits! Endure the pain!!

Today I woke up shaking, sweat-covered, in a deep, melancholy mood. I heard the orderly screaming down the hall to get in line for morning meds. I slid on my grey sticky socks and sweat shirt, looked at myself in the mirror, and slumped my way out the door. The others were standing in line, some looking down, some looking up and smiling, but mostly all of us minding our own business in this place for the disturbed and mentally distraught. I took my pills and prepared for the morning breakfast, all the time thinking about what brought me to this lowly state; a highly decorated soldier, a drill instructor, a leader and warrior by trade, a lifelong soldier, in a hospital for the mentally insane. I shook it off and splashed my face with cold water from the sink. My eyes were bloodshot from the night of torment in my head. I slid my jeans on and then looked at the bible my wife had left me with all the verses marked and highlighted. I left it there as I went to breakfast.

As we formed up for morning breakfast all the soldiers grouped together, and all the other kind of mentally ill patients left the soldiers alone. We did stay together in this place. No one told us to; it was just the way it was. A team is never broken, no matter where you are. There are PVTs (privates) trying to get out of basic here. I tried to stay out of their way and not expose myself as a drill instructor, so I didn't shave and let my hair grow long. I was here for me, not them. I let them smoke my cigarettes and never once let them know I was in charge. I didn't want to be a leader here; I was far from it at this point in time. Everything in my life was falling apart. How could I help someone when I couldn't even help myself?

Later in the day we all sat in the "circle of trust" in the group, and I talked about the big push in September 2004. The counselor tried to use art therapy. We were supposed to draw a picture of our nightmare. The first picture was the one picture in our minds that kept us awake at night, then draw the picture that we wanted the most to come true. My Crayola markers came to life as I bore down, and with tears dripping on the paper I drew a very vivid picture of a battle scene on the bridge near CP-31 in Abu-Graib. Once I was done with the battle scene, I shifted gears and went directly to what my heart desired: A picture of my family, a big house, kids, my wife, dogs, cats, sun, etc. Everyone in the group started to explain their pictures. It was my turn. I held up the pictures, and a gasp was heard through the room. The counselor came and patted my shoulder. She explained all the pain she saw in both pictures. I didn't understand. "How could there be pain in both pictures?" I asked. She said one was obvious, but the family picture was not colored; it was all in black and white. That meant that the family was still very far away and that I have not returned home yet from the war. I was staggered by such an assessment. I was only in the center for one day. She hit me like a Mack truck. I sat back in my chair and thought to myself, "I must be in the right place."

While giving thought to the group study of the day, a million questions were racing through my mind. The images of the war were stronger then they had ever been before. I had for sure not returned home. I was still fighting in my dreams, and in my waking hours. I used the computer to find peace, I think. I tried everything to find peace. My addictions are not because I don't love my wife; they are just because the pain is just too great. I can't find a cork to stop the flow of agony.

The Army has rules for this kind of pain, though, especially us guys being in the Infantry: "Suck it up...Drive on...No pain...You can take it...You're weak minded...This is just a phase you're going through...Your head will get right soon enough..All of this will pass with time, Soldier." I know this is a shock to all of you, but I am not a robot. I'm just so tired nowadays. I'm tired of what the Army wants me to be. I want my life back, I want my wife back, and I want my kids back. <u>I want to come home!</u>

I'm still trying to figure out why I can't trust anyone as I sit here and write in this book. I look around this room and see sadness. I'm in the right place. Misery loves company. It's so black here that the darkness just flows out of this room. I threw my family away to try to be the perfect soldier. I set boundaries and walls. I set blinders to the world that is around me. The only place I really knew where I was on the desert floor. I want to trust Jen again with all these feelings and emotions, but for some reason it is difficult to tell my wife all of this, of what I am going through.

When I left Baghdad the last time, I cried. I didn't understand why we were leaving when the job wasn't done. Still, we believed overall in the goodness of our cause. What good could it have been now? We killed lots of bad guys and plenty of civilians. We left plenty of brothers on the streets of Baghdad. How could we agree to line the rich's pockets while we poor men choose to die? Out of 120 of us, 40 got wounded and sent home, 3 KIA. Out of our platoon alone, 12 PH and half sent home. Yet the job wasn't done!

DAY 3, 29SEPT2007

> Take a breath, Soldier. What do you
> see? The screams of the wounded
> haunt my dreams. The tip of the sword
> is dull. Have to find balance. A man
> can't serve two masters! Which one
> does your soul belong to now, Soldier?

Today I talked to another doctor, and I let him read my journal entries. Like many old warriors before me, he took a more philosophical view of all this pain inside my head. Once again the doctor said it was time for me to start the healing process. While I was talking to him my mind started to drift back to Abu-Graib. I could hear the cries of the wounded, wounded civilians on CP-12, and his face started to disappear as the faces of the dead lying around the destroyed minivan clouded the conversation. His voice was muffled as the radio in my track started to blare louder and louder. I could feel the heat on my face and feel the sand and dust in my lungs again. Along with the burning minivan the blood choked the air in the little room where we were talking. The wounded cries, of civilians being put on the back of my track in Arabic started to overwhelm me as I started to shake. The doctor snapped his fingers. I looked at him and said nothing. This meeting was over. He let me go back to my room.

After the morning meeting, I went back to my room. I picked up my Bible and begged for God to relieve my agony. I can't help but feel that people think these feelings I am having are for the weak minded. I told my counselor just a couple of minutes ago that I felt like a broken piece of machinery, a spoke spinning around in a broken wheel. I've felt like this for so long now that it is hard to feel anything else. I want to feel happiness again; however, it eludes me. I cry on my knees alone at night in this grey, locked-down room, alone. Panic fills my mind here, in this place of darkness. I smell the streets every waking second. I feel as if I can't function on the line anymore at my Unit. I hurt, I suffer, and yet I can't find the peace to put all this behind me, even though I try. I play it all off to those around me as if I'm playing some sick game, hiding the truth of my bleakness. I try to keep going, all the while feeling as if I'm drowning with my hands above the water, begging for help but can't speak. All the while I'm sitting here, dying from the inside out.

Another couple of hours go by. I look forward to getting this treatment over with and really coming home and seeing Jen. Even here I can't manage enough energy to stand or even move. I'm consistently tired, exhausted, continuously fighting a battle in my mind that seems to never end. Standing up now or getting out of bed is a challenge for me at this point in time. My depression has reached a new stage, and I have no idea how far down it will go. I just don't want to do anything right now.

Guilt is my driving force right now. I want to love Jen, but I have been gone so much and done so many horrific things in my career that I don't think my love for her or her love for me could ever recover. I used to make excuses about this condition and play it off. I am finally ready to stop the running. I don't want to live with the quilt of my excuses anymore. I want to be happy. I want to feel again. I want to look into her eyes and feel her love. I want her to be able to see love in my eyes in return.

DAY 4, 30SEPT2007

> Separation of
> reality...Who has that
> in this world of pain?!

Today was a good day. My wife and kids came to visit. Surprisingly, Jen brought everyone to see me, and they all understood why I am here in this mental hospital.

Jen and I talked, and she said I should not take the whole of the responsibilities of what brought me here from the Army on my shoulders. I asked for help months ago before I got out of control. However, that still doesn't change the fact that I dishonored myself, my family, my corps, and my Army. I should have had better control of my actions than what I did. I should not have had committed the crime I did that they are charging me with. For many in the service it is simple: Make a choice. However, for us, those who are afflicted with this disease, it is not so simple. A lifetime of dedication to an Army that has become my family has just been flushed away. I stood in front of many men and taught them about Army values, and yet I couldn't even live up to the very thing I taught. I feel like such a hypocrite.

Once again, in my mind I couldn't separate reality from the storm. Everything is confused now. The raw emotion has taken over, just like in Baghdad. It is time for survival, fight or die. I left a piece of my soul over there; now fight to get it back or let go. That is what the Army doesn't understand. My achievements have been a mask for my darkness, and my failures for my weakness. I have finally hit my bottom. I can't get any lower. Maybe it is time to finally give the Army the answer they want: Early retirement for this old soldier.

DAY 5-6, 1-2OCT2007

> The war machine = A pine box.
>
> We march in one after another, blissfully obeying the orders of those above us, trying to solve a problem that can't be solved.

Yesterday I had a better day. Jen and the boys visited. Her understanding of the situation is beyond anything I could have asked of her. After all I put her through during the war and countless deployments overseas; she is still by my side. She is unbelievable. I have told her all my sins over the last couple of months, and yet she still stands by me. Letting her know all my sins made me more depressed, because I know she doesn't deserve me and can do a hell of a lot better. She tries to make a comfortable house. She tries and I destroy all that love with my actions. This latest thing, the hospital, is just one more thing to add on to my loser list of things that she should leave me for, but she says she is behind me once again a hundred percent. How someone can love another so much is beyond anything I have ever seen in my world travels.

After they left I felt good for the first time in years. I had my first good thought about the war in years too. It was about the primary elections. How hundreds of thousands of people came out to route huskies and walked it. Unafraid of terrorism, they walked to vote for their freedom. It was a brief thought of happiness…then I walked back to my grey room and prepared for the nightly psych classes.

This morning started out really rough. All the patients seemed like they all lined up in front of my door and ambushed me with questions about the war. I had been in the hospital for five days now, and they have left me alone until now. That is how I liked it, solitary in my grief and misery, but this morning all of the civilians here had other plans.

One guy cornered me on the smoke break. He was in for chemical dependency. He just flat out asked if we were winning the war over there. I answered back, "Which fight?" He seemed confused by this question. In my mind and in anybody else's mind who served over there, the answer is clear. Baghdad and Afghanistan are two totally different animals.

He asked again. I started to panic at his persistence. I really couldn't answer that question clearly. It was two years since my last tour. The press says it's better; but in my gut I knew it wasn't. I knew how the press and the government kept America in the dark about all that went on in Iraq. I could only speak about what I saw and did. This guy wanted an answer about the now, and I only had the past. I felt the heat on my face again and heard the bullets whistling over my head. I smelled the staleness of the sand, and I stood there in silence as he pressed his question again. For the whole smoke break he stood by me as I clocked out of reality, trying to hold on to my composure and not kill this guy that had no clue what he was asking. I saw the market again and the street corner where we were always attacked, and wished I wasn't there. I felt every emotion again and prayed that this guy would just leave me alone. I wanted to punch him and just scream at the top of my lungs. My hands started to tremble as my mind and face became stone. I took a breath and answered his question with emotionless tears running down my face. "We are losing this fight in Iraq!" I walked away shaking. For the first time, I told a civilian what I truly felt in my heart about the war in Iraq, and it felt horrible. I felt so dirty that I didn't want to continue on with the rest of the day's activities.

DAY 7, 3OCT2007

> I KILLED THEM!!!!!!!
>
> I SHOULD HAVE SHOT,
>
> I SHOULD HAVE SHOT!!!
>
> STOP THE PAIN IN MY HEAD!

Last night was horrible. At group I talked about the incident in the market. It was about 1730 (5:30 p.m.) and the market in Abu-Graib was starting to close down for the evening. My section had a tour of duty at a fire base called Raider Base. This is where we launched a lot of our counter recon patrols and light-foot patrols. Pretty much anything we could think of we launched from there. Plus, we had an additional task of watching the market from static positions with thermal night vision systems to keep it safe and a clear route for civilians and military traffic.

It was my shift on the thermals overlooking the market. I noticed something a little strange by one of the wooden bamboo shacks on the left side of the market. There were four men. They showed up clearly in my thermals moving around behind a shed that had been empty for a bit. I zoomed in. They were messing around with something. Still unsure, I watched for about five minutes as the market continued to empty. Finally a large-built man stepped out from behind the shed, got on his belly and started to push a box in front of him. Immediately I knew what it was. A roadside bomb was getting put into place. I scanned back to the other men behind him and watched as they were stringing out the wire behind him. This was the first time I actually saw a bomb getting laid in...A golden opportunity to engage the enemy first, instead of getting hit first. I armed my system and got on the radio to my infantry fire team on top of the roof behind me and told them to follow my tracer in. When I start to shoot, send everything they got upstairs down on top of the area I'm engaging. They complied with the order.

The mood was getting more intense as sweat rolled down my face. The man was getting closer to the road. Over the radio I called battalion on a net call and advised all the foot patrols and light observation posts (OPs) to take cover, because a Bradley was about to engage targets on the left side of the market. I sent the grid, armed my system, and was about to engage when my radio crackled, "Seize fire." I stopped and let my finger off the trigger. By that time the man was at the side of the road now and was turning around, still on his belly.

Battalion said for me not to fire, that they were sending a light fire team that was in a close observation post to capture the bad guys that were lying in the bomb. I protested emphatically that it was too late and that the bomb was already set, plus I had a clear shot and was ready to engage. I was ordered not to fire and to guide the men in on top of the bad guys. I grew sick to my stomach. I knew with all my heart I should engage and disobey that order. These men were going in blind. Even with my guidance, they still had no idea what was going on. The danger was just doubled by fifty. I asked again if I could engage. Again I was told no. By now elements were moving on the objective, and I was to hold my fire.

I looked in the area again and saw them coming. Those poor guys would not know what hit them. I tried to tell them to back up, that they were right on top of the bomb as the enemy escaped up another route away from the maneuvering elements. Just as I said, "Back up, back UP!" the bomb blew. Their bodies flew through the air. I saw the blast and the smoke and the dust, and then nothing left. "God-damit!" I screamed over the net. I fucking knew it! I threw my helmet off and went to the back of my track and puked. I was so mad at that time, and the tears just started rolling. I couldn't control myself. I wanted to go back to Battalion and kill the man who made that decision.

I killed them!! It is my fault. I can't live with this pain!! I had the enemy in my sights and I let them go. I had the enemy in my sights, and I let them go!!! I cried all night long in this dark, grey room of pain.

DAY 8, 4OCT2007

> The first step is the hardest.
>
> Be realistic in your goals.

Jen and the boys came by last night. I enjoyed that visit very much. The boys were more talkative tonight than they ever were before on previous visits. I believe they enjoyed the visit as well. For the first time since I have been in this place, I was just Dale, not Drill SGT. I felt like someone legitimately loved me for who I was deep inside, instead of the false bravado the last year and half produced. The boys seemed like they cared and were concerned for my condition as well as for my well-being. Their actions truly spoke louder than their words did last night, and I had a lot to think about as I lay down to sleep.

Today I thought I had a moment of clarity as to why I am here and what has been going on in my head since the first time I arrived at the treatment center. On one of the smoke breaks, I was talking to one of the Vietnam Veterans and some of the other Veterans that were in here. They flat out told me that I just have to deal with the pain of war, that it doesn't go away and I would have to live with this agony forever and also that the pain never ends. While I was sitting there listening to their stories and sympathizing with them, because I have never forgotten the freedoms other service members have given me for freedom, I noticed their colored bands on their arms. The colored bands mark you while you're in the treatment facility. Mine was for mental health issues, of   course, so I was green, yellow was for chemical dependency, and pink was for both. The guy who was talking to me had all of them. Something that I noticed with all the vets was the fact that they all had chemical dependency on their wrist. I asked one about it, and he said it was easier to deal with the pain of war through drugs and alcohol. All of my doctors and therapists are shocked to find out that I put down the bottle after the first Gulf War in 1991, after it damned near killed me and destroyed my marriage. They are shocked I'm still married after all my tours. They're shocked I still am not in trouble for drugs or did any hard time, and they're even more shocked that I haven't knocked myself off yet.

So my moment of clarity was this. If these guys after 20 some-odd years are still having problems, I better get it straight. It is not wrong to want help. It is not wrong to want to feel alive again, to love my wife and kids again, to become undetached and get reattached to the world. The Army was a good life for awhile and it gave me a good start, but now there has to be something more than war out there for me. I want a life outside of all this violence. I want my wife and kids back. I have given Jen and the boys a life through my sacrifice, not a good one by any means but good enough.

To finally connect with my wife and kids again, I can't continue to think that this is all going to get worse and that the pain will last forever. If it does, I would kill myself. How do I cope with this every day and survive if it continues to get worse?

I have to let go of my vulnerabilities to everything and stop living on the tip of the sword. Once I do that it will let Jen in, and then it will let everything else in. It will open up the flood gates of raw emotion. That however, will be a new step for me in this life of pain and suffering, but I think it would truly be a step in the right direction. It is never wrong to love someone and want the same love in return. I have to drop my walls.

DAY 9, 5OCT2007

> The real spin: Our soldiers
> train for 9 weeks, the Iraqi
> Army trains for 6 years.
>
> Stop the pain!! The U.S. Agenda
> is to stay in Baghdad.

Today I am exhausted. I started the day off sick to my stomach. We all lined up like we were supposed to see the doctor for our morning, shrinking heads session. He told me this morning that the attack in Abu-Graib that night was because of God, and I had no blame in the fact that those men died the way they did. That was easy for him to say. I felt my finger on the trigger as he talked. Instantly my mind drifted. I snapped back very angry this time. How dare he tell me how I felt! We were a brotherhood over there. If you've never been there then you wouldn't understand why I felt so bad. Who does this head shrinker think he is? I got madder as my face started to show displeasure in his conversation.

"My ROEs (Rules of Engagement) were specific," I blurted out. "Even though I was pulled off the target, it was still my responsibility to protect men, or any soldier for that matter, around me. PERIOD!" I yelled.

The interview for the morning visit was quickly over after that. How can I explain to a man who has never been there the pain of losing comrades in battle? It just cannot be done. As I walked away I kept saying to myself, "I should have disobeyed that order." It would have been easier to go to a court martial. The ROE was put in place for those decisions. There should have been no hesitation; there should have been no question. Plus, if there is any doubt and you pull the trigger the ROE will fall into place when the investigation is done. You pull the damn trigger.

I walked to the window far in the back and started to cry again as I watched the rain fall on Kentucky through the triple-pained, wired glass of the mental hospital. I started to question myself as a good soldier again. It was my job to put the bad guys down. Maybe things would have been different if I would have shot. Ifs, buts, and however, are for the weak minded, and an infantryman is never weak minded in the field. My men and I fought hard for that small section of Abu-Graib. We take a street one day, the enemy would have it back by the next morning. Every single day it seemed like we were fighting the same fights over and over again. The enemy didn't stop; they kept coming and coming. Car bombs, road side bombs, snipers, RPGs, and everything else they could throw at us they did. The enemy would hit you and fade into the crowd. You felt surrounded every single day you were on patrol.

So when you had the chance to kill some of those bastards, you took it. You didn't wait around for approval. It is the job of every soldier that is in theater to protect their buddies to their left and right regardless of race, creed, or religion and that night I failed in my job.

I saw them lay out that bomb, for God's sake. I had the shot. We didn't build schools there. We didn't help with the electrical supply. Fighting was all we knew there. We were there to go into those suburbs of Baghdad in 04-05 and bring order and destroy the militias tearing them apart. Not to satisfy some political quota. We were engaged every day, 15-hour patrols some days.

As I stood there crying, watching the rain while the thoughts of the past raced through my head, I thought that it wasn't the killing part of the job that I had a problem with all these years later. It was my inability to stop the enemy that always got to me. I felt like a rolling target that made me this way. Give me a straight-up fight any day of the week. I would take that more than that sneaky, un-honorable way they fought us there. We were the hunted, not the hunters, and finding the enemy in that urban jungle was almost impossible for what my Unit was used too.

So you don't tie soldiers' hands. When they have the shot, you let them take it.

The real spin: My self-interpretation, a continual circle of death that never will end.

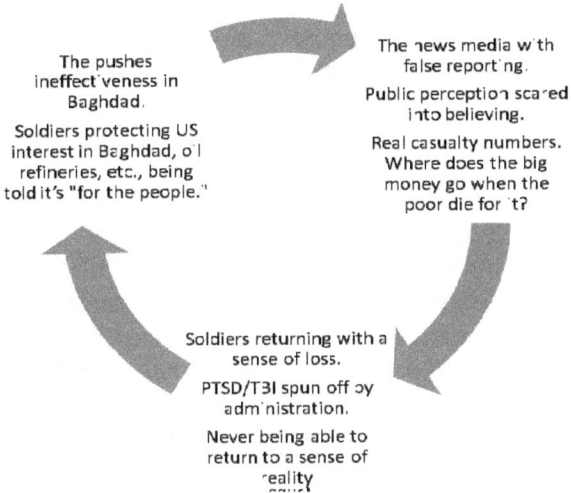

The pushes ineffect'veness in Baghdad.

Soldiers protecting US interest in Baghdad, o'l refineries, etc., being told it's "for the people."

The news media w'th false report'ng.

Public perception sca'ed into believing.

Real casualty numbers. Where does the big money go when the poor die for 't?

Soldiers returning with a sense of loss.

PTSD/T3I spun off oy adm'nistration.

Never being able to return to a sense of reality

DAY 10-11, 7-8OCT2007

> Am I starting to get better in this
> place with my brother crazies??

The last two days have been the roughest yet. I thought I was making headway on my recovery, but I'm still exhausted and having flashbacks for the majority of the day.

Roommates come and go here in this place. When the doctor feels you're good enough to be released, you're released back into the world. So far I'd had three. Yesterday I got a new one. A soldier, brand new to the Army, still going through basic training. I didn't mind, even if I was still a Drill Instructor. He was older, about mid 30s, so that helped out. He didn't talk much, but he couldn't control his emotions. I thought *I* was bad. Continuous shaking and crying, plus an intense rage that made him throw his head into the wall all the time. After one night of this I decided I'd had enough of that. I remembered Jen had left me my Bible. She brought it by with some smokes and other things I requested for my stay.

The Bible, black leather, was worn on the binding from all the tours of duty I went on. It was sitting on my desk. I hadn't looked at it in 2 years, not since I returned home from the war. God and I weren't exactly on speaking terms after I got back. I just placed it on the shelf and let it collect dust. Jen dusted it off for me and brought it in here. I guess she figured this was a good time to get reacquainted. I walked over to it. It was past lights out, and the floor was silent except for my roommate, who was in one of his anxiety attacks.

Exhausted from the day's mental health evals and groups, I picked it up. I started flipping through the familiar passages again. I went right to Psalm 69:

"Save me, O God,

For the waters have come up to my neck.

I sink in the miry depths."

"You know I am disgraced and scorned, all my enemies are before Thee,

I looked for sympathy and there was none,

for comforters and found none."

I read the whole passage to him and watched as his rage turned to calm. His tears turned to silence, and his heavy breathing became more relaxed. Eventually in the passage David praises God for giving him the strength to carry on with his tormentors. As I read, calm came over me as well. I couldn't explain it. I didn't want to. All that mattered at that time was that two people who were having some issues found a small bit of heaven in the most unlikely place on the planet. Just for a brief second, we both found peace. We were brothers in pain in need of healing at that time, and PVT or not we both were going to get some sleep that night.

This morning I was summoned by a doctor I never met before. I guess the Army needed a full-blown diagnosis about my condition, and that is why he was there. We talked all morning. He asked about situations in combat, home, and in the Army. All of them were hard questions to answer, especially all the questions about the fighting. He explained that he had worked with combat vets for over 20 years with severe PTSD, and he was there to see if had it.

I went through a battery of tests, and by the end of it my mind was fried. My nerves were like firecrackers going off in my head. I couldn't stop crying. He got what he wanted, all right: An honest and open assessment of me and who I am. Later on in the same interview he stopped it and said there was no need to continue. In his professional opinion I had it, and all he had to do now was to put it on paper. So I filled out somewhere around a 500-hundred-word questionnaire about my emotions. I came to find out later that I was depressed and emotionally unstable. I laughed when I heard that. No kidding! I could have saved them some money and just told them that. In case you haven't figured it out yet, I have severe PTSD, major depression, and a couple of other things going on. It only took them a day to get the results back. I did give them permission to share that with the Army. It would explain a lot as to why I committed and the crime they're charging me with.

This is not a title I am very happy with at all. I tried for several years after the fighting to control my feelings and emotions, to hide my true feelings with horrible habits, to become emotionally lost, to leave my soul in Baghdad…just to wonder why, when the darkness closed, in how come I was going out of my mind. The depression was so great at times that even the thought of my wife and kids saving me like they normally did didn't matter to me. This confused my counselors to no end. They are shocked that I haven't shot anybody yet. I guess the answer to that is because of my wife and kids, even though I put them at risk now with this crime.

I tried to live up to the corps I loved in the Army, the husband I wanted to be, plus a great father. But failure followed in my footsteps. The only place where I knew I could succeed was the field of battle. Everything was easier there. Even when it wasn't easy, we still knew what we had to do. Here the emotions overwhelm me, control my thoughts. My actions were and are out of control.

Therein lies the problem with me. I guess I trusted the Army so much that when I asked for help and didn't get it, I crashed and continued down my destructive path.

Once again, I went to my favorite window and looked out at the swirling storm whipping at the trees and the lightning on the horizon, reminding me of an upcoming invasion because of artillery lighting up the darkest nights in cities far away. I crossed my arms and bowed my head. I closed my eyes. When does this pain end?

DAY 12, 8OCT2007

> Gunner Co-Ax troop! Fire, hit him! Hit
> him! Adjust fire! Good kill. Shift fire
> right! Fire, fire, fire!!!!!!

Last night I really couldn't sleep. I woke up hour after hour. I had a nightmare again. It was in my memory like someone choking the life out of me. I was getting crushed under my own mental weight and would wake up in a panic. I dreamed I was back in Baghdad again, riding around and waiting to get hit like we always did. All of a sudden the ambush started. First it was RPGs, then roadside bombs, then small arms fire. As the fight continued, I was on the radio with my higher headquarters telling them what was going on. As the wounded started to pile up, my headquarters wanted a grid to my location so they could send backup. As I reached for my Garmin GPS it wasn't there. The wounded started to cry more and there wasn't a medic in sight. (My Garmin was a gift from my wife while I was over there. It had all of my grid and my sector on it, check points, MedEvac points, gates, routes, almost everything you could think of). My Garmin survived several engagements with the enemy, and it wasn't there. The screams of the wounded got louder and louder, and the fight got even deadlier. I literally didn't know where I was.

The enemy had closed the distance, and hand-to-hand fighting started. I reached for my double-bladed knife my boys bought me, and that wasn't their either. My weapon jammed, and I had to use it defensively like I taught my men on a refresher course of rifle close-in fighting techniques. I had no map, no ammo, no medic, no knife, and didn't know where I was. I woke up in a cold sweat breathing hard. The nurse said I was screaming for people to get to cover and fighting her in my sleep. My roommate even said they were going to call people and pin me to the bed. They gave me sleeping pills, but that just seemed to make the nightmares worse. I woke up at 2, 3, 4, and 5. When I have my nightmares, it is always best that people leave me alone. I had to put a sign on my door. "If asleep, please call to me from the doorway". That way none of the nurses in the hospital got hurt. It's time to go to group, and I'm exhausted from struggling all night.

#

Today in group we talked about being able to cope with the outside world. You know, our families, jobs, kids, etc. I know Jen and the boys are waiting for me to get out of this place. That is the only happiness I can find in my life right now. My depression hurts so bad right now that it is difficult to even see the good in them. I know that my career in the Infantry is definitely over with the diagnosis of severe PTSD. That is a hard blow to handle, but to be honest with you, I'm glad. I served 18 years as a grunt and I served well. I have many mental and physical scars to prove it. I have a good start on a Bachelor's degree. I have served my country proudly, and I don't think anyone any place can deny me that. It's just the fact of getting an early retirement that is surreal to me. For the longest time I sacrificed all I could for my country, putting it first over everything and above all others. Now I want more. But now it is difficult to let go of what I have done for so many years. It is difficult to see the future past tomorrow. I have never been so lost in my career until now. How could I possibly make it on the outside?

I am institutionalized in the Army system now. I don't know anything else.

My reality has always been safer in war zones and overseas. I've been away so much; how could I possibly get out of the military with this disability and start clean with my family? What kind of struggles would that bring? I sink deeper in my depression when I think of all that could have been in my career and what I have done in my career. There is an eternal loneliness that comes with being a soldier. I look out the barred windows in my room here in this mental hospital and feel the heat of the sniper bullet going by my head sometimes. Sometimes I look out and smell the sand and hear the choppers above with the rumbling of my track beneath my feet. Then I close my eyes and hear voices from the past: My friends, my comrades, alive and dead. I pray to God to give me strength. How can I fight this? I can't fight something I can't see, this affliction that is killing me. I feel Baghdad as I look out the window, and once again the ghost of my past and foreboding near-future make me cry again in my room.

DAY 13, 9OCT2007

> Fallen brothers – <u>YOU ARE NOT</u>
> <u>FORGOTTEN</u>!!

    Another rough day today. This morning once again I was cornered about the war. Someone asked is it true that they have wires strung across the roads to cut your heads off when you drive by. Instantly I went back to me and my gunner standing up, flying down Route Huskies, and the track pin we put in our flag holders to catch the piano wire the enemy strung across the top of the road. We caught a piece of piano wire one day that was strung track high from pole to pole. The track pin broke the wire and shattered it. At 25 mph, the pin wire would have cut both our heads off. Nothing needed to be said; My gunner and I looked at each other like so many times before and just shook our heads.

    In the courtyard, there is a brick wall here at the hospital. When I walk outside to smoke, I look at the bricks and remember how our A-Co would park their patrol in this same spot every day. It was a big mistake. There was an open field of rubble to the north we called the kill zone as we drove by every day. We always got engaged from this kill zone. Sometimes from IED's, RPGs, snipers you name it the enemy would set up shop in this rubble area. So a light patrol of Infantry went in there daily to make sure it was clear. There was a massive brick wall down the little dirt trail entrance, and they stopped the same way they always do. The enemy disguised two 155 artillery rounds in the brick. The enemy was cleaver that way. It really looked like brick. Well it ripped through them when the enemy triggered it. It killed 3 of them instantly and destroyed 2 Humvees.

Then I talked about a call we went on once again. A-Co was on a foot patrol, and they got hit. They needed a MedEvac quick, and we arrived. Well, this soldier was looking in a hole, and for some reason that his squad leader did not understand, he jumped in it. The enemy triggered the secondary bomb. The only thing left of him was his torso protected by his plates; everything else was gone. We wrapped him in a poncho and put him in the back of the track. We took him to the nearest CSH (Combat Support Hospital, "cash"). Two days later another patrol found his boots with his feet still in them.

DAY 14, 11 OCT2007 - Release Day

> ### I CAN'T TURN OFF THE SWITCH!
>
> Shoot everything that moves! Action Left! Fire!
> Contact left! Step to the side, Fire! Action Right!
> Action Front! Contact Right! Engage! Engage!
> Engage! On my order FIRE! Pivot and fire! Keep
> working! Z-pattern, Z-pattern! Keep moving!
> Turn left! Fire! Fire! Fire!

I was released from the hospital today. Kind of an ominous sign, Jen had a blowout on the way to get me. I wasn't really worried, though. She has never let me down before.

I was scared today. I didn't know what would happen when I got home, but home was home. I quickly went in and hugged all the kids. The soldiers at the hospital cried when I left. I do believe for some reason I have the ability to lead men without hardly doing anything to impress them. It still amazes me how everyone I have contact with seems to pull towards me.

There was this one guy in the hospital, very violent. He approached me and asked for a fight. I stood there and contemplated his question and said, "You want to roll? OK. But I'm telling you now, nothing you have ever done will compare to the violence I will inflict on you. Plus, after I'm down I put your head under the pavement!" He came in with shackles and cuffs on the first day he arrived at the hospital. Surprisingly, he and I became very close, and because I'm criminology major I offered him a different career path, one that he would be suitable doing. He called the company I mentioned, and he has an interview as soon as he is done with county jail.

This is a perplexing problem for me. Even when I was hospitalized, men in the psych ward still followed me. I can help everybody else, but I can't seem to help myself most of the time.

I have started today, the long road home! It is paved with obstacles, but I'm ready. BRING IT!!

NO PAIN – JUST HEALING!

DAY 15, 12 OCT2007 – PATH (Positive Approach to Healing) Group

Today was the day I dreaded the most. I stood outside the door of the PATH group. A group that is outpatient at the Army hospital for combat vets recovering with PTSD and TBI. I stood their staring at the door as all the as all of the Vets piled in. Laughing and talking about RPGs and the enemies that they engaged. I felt sick to my stomach and almost puked right there in the hallway. My hands started to shake, and sweat poured off my forehead. Another infantryman came to the door. I recognized him right away. He was another Drill Instructor from my sister unit. I went on many joint missions with him, and I was glad to see his face although I was not glad about the circumstances. He smiled and said, "Welcome. I know all about it." I stepped through the doorway and inched my towards a seat in the corner. The counselor came in. I was pleased to see all the ranks represented in the group from Master SGT on down. They all had several tours down range. That, however, brought me no comfort. As the group started, the counselor put in a movie about PTSD, and it showed images of the war. I about threw up. All of the flashbacks hit me all at once. I found myself back in Baghdad and on the Saudi floor. All of the images of the dead raced through my head. I was shaking so bad the group had to stop. I apologized. Of course, they all tried to comfort me. I had to leave the room immediately.   I almost didn't go back. I felt like a piece of discarded equipment. I didn't feel that I was worth saving at that point. The pain was just too great. I only keep breathing, the technique they taught me at the hospital, and prayed that Jen would come and rub my back and tell me it was all right. I was home!

Change of Duty Position

After the group I went and picked up Jen, and we went to the Unit. We stopped and got doughnuts and coffee. She had tears in her eyes when she got back in the car. I asked what was wrong. She said we are celebrating Doug's life. I used to have to get my Captain doughnuts and coffee, kind of a running joke at IOBC where I taught officers for 2 years. (More to follow about Doug.)

We went to the Unit and found that my picture was taken off the wall, and I found the 1SG. We sat there, and he asked how I was, no explanation about why they didn't come and see me in the hospital. He called the CSM (Command SGT Major), and we were off to see him. Almost 3 weeks had gone by with no explanation as to my punishment. I thought that this was the reading of my preliminary Article 15, or court martial. He calmed me down, and he explained that my job was to heal and not worry about anything else. He pulled me from the drill sergeant line and assigned me to the S3 until a conclusion could be made on my status.

I went back to the Unit and emptied out my wall locker with Jen. As I was packing I couldn't help but think about how lost I was and how I failed myself at the Unit. I became a ghost in a Battalion I cherished. Jen asked me if anyone from the Company would call me on my cell. I looked at her and said, "No one will call."

> A shadow...Left behind...An empty shell...The ghost...
>
> Battle Buddy is only half the word.

DAY 17, 14 OCT2007

> ACCEPT THEIR LOVE!
>
> DON'T WITHDRAW
> FROM YOUR SAFE
> PLACE!!
>
> LOVE = JEN & BOYS
>
> FOCUS BLUE!
>
> FOCUS NO PAIN!

Today was a good day, even though I got an e-mail from a buddy in Baghdad who's in the 3rd ID. Steve and I had been through tours in Korea. He is a Platoon SGT on his 4th tour. I worry about him every day.

I guess I can talk about Doug today. His rank and full name are of no concern, but the people who stood around Doug were truly blessed. He was my boss at IOBC. He helped me to get instructor of the cycle twice. His knowledge of infantry tactics was amazing, and we made a good team. I could lead, and he dealt with more of the tactical planning. A truly amazing man.

Doug always had a great sense of humor and always made me buy coffee for him, mainly because he said his alimony was breaking him. I always laughed at that one. He gave me leeway to train the finest officers on the planet. That was unheard of at IOBC. Doug always said, "You train them and teach them everything you know." He let me design training above the standard training plan.

On October 30, 2006, I sat down by my computer to work on my classes. I got an e-mail from a officer I trained. He stated that the Major was KIA (killed in action) in a road side bomb ambush in Afghanistan. I went numb as the tears flowed. Jen asked why I was crying and saw the e-mail. That made 22 LTs and three Majors I loved KIA's. They all went to Arlington.

At the group and at the hospital, they say I haven't allowed myself to grieve. I'm still in the denial stage of grief. I just can't accept that God would allow the best America has to offer to die in this horrible war.

WHY THEM, GOD?! WHY?! WHY?!!

MEN, YOU ARE NOT FORGOTTEN – I'LL SALUTE YOU

IN HEAVEN!!

DAY 19, 17OCT2007

Today was a relatively rough day, even though I really didn't do anything. We went to a prayer lunch with the Chaplain. He must have known I was coming, because his topic was how people could become very bitter because of their situations in life. I thought that to be very ironic.

How can I <u>not</u> be bitter about a war with such loss, personal loss, marital loss and parental loss? I came back here from Iraq so demoralized about what we did there, and seeing all the stuff I saw changed me forever.

I have been bitter, devastatingly so. I try every day to put it all behind me. I struggle daily to find happiness and accept the loss of my brothers. I struggle to understand the humanity in all this madness.

Jen has been my battle buddy. Some call that co-dependence, but I call it sticking it out in a marriage when times get tough. Right now, the Army has the highest divorce rate in American history.

Keeping myself together some days is almost more than I can stand. I still feel left behind. The Army is going to do what is right by me, even though a lot of folks might not agree with the litigation about to happen.

My head hurts constantly. Sometimes it's very hard for me to remember anything. It's hard for me to concentrate. It's difficult some days to even think I am accepting everything that has happened to me.

I look forward to finally finding peace.

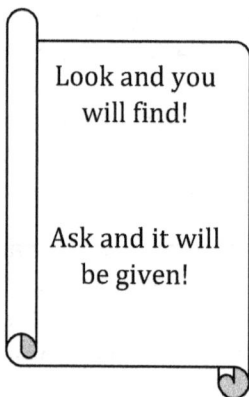

Look and you
will find!

Ask and it will
be given!

DAY 20, 18OCT2007

Today in group we talked about controlling our anger. In life I guess you do what you have to do. They put this model on the board:

I accept this situation.

I may not like it.

It hurts the situation I'm in,

But I can't control it,

So let it go.

That is very hard for a man who has set aside his whole life in defense of his country. There have been bad calls in Baghdad. Trust me, I've been on the receiving end of most of them. As a SGT, how do you displace the reality on the ground from a guy sitting in the rear, telling you how to do your job when he doesn't see the things the way you do.

I should have shot. That is the harsh reality; however, I did what I was trained to do: Follow orders. Did it suck? Yes, it did. Did it hurt? Yes, it did. Was I turned off from feelings after that? Yes, I was.

This brings me to another point, the feelings of intimacy. It's not sexual, but I hear all the time from Vets that they loved their soldiers and job more than they loved their wives.

It is trust that your friend will save you, a trust that only men who have been to combat share. It's a bond built by blood. We said if we could take our wives and let them get shot and save them, then we would have true intimacy with them.

My struggle is exactly that: Trying to regain intimacy with everyone in my family; trust, a safe place, being home, understanding the difference in reality.

I'm not in Baghdad, I'm not on a street in Abu-Graib, I'm not leading men into battle. Perception has to change in order for me to get better. The fact is, I'm a soldier, expected to put the mission first and family last, and I can't do that anymore.

DAY 21-22OCT2007

Yesterday started off badly. The tankers were firing their big guns close to our house on base, so I decided to go to the mental hospital and talk to the guys I knew there. I wore my uniform. They cried, smiled, laughed and hugged when they saw me. The bad day turned to good. It was a good thing to tell the PVTs that they weren't alone, and they loved the visit. Even if they weren't my soldiers, it meant a lot to have another soldier show them that type of respect when they were down.

Jen and I started talking about how I always put everything first. I have to agree. Even when I was in my darkest hours, I still excelled in my duty positions. I find it amazing that even with all those thoughts in my head I was still able to concentrate.

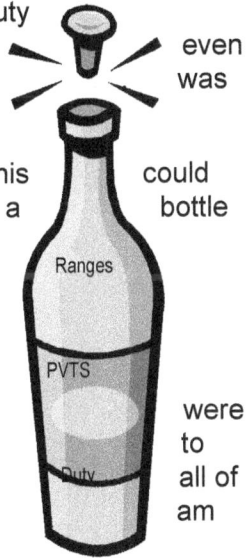

Everyone is wondering how this could have happened to me. It's like taking a bottle and filling it up with emotion and trying to cap it with a cork. You keep filling it up until you explode with all those emotions. This is a breeding ground for depression and high anxiety. All the signs for my crash were there; it's just that I didn't have time to acknowledge the pressure. I avoided all of it through sexual deviance, which I am ashamed of deeply. I thought I could control my actions, but unfortunately the escape from reality controlled me.

I am having a very difficult time accepting the family and life realities away from war. I knew guys who volunteered to go back time and time again. That is their comfort of reality. I don't understand how war could be comforting at all.

Perception of my reality is skewed between over there and over here. However, Jen has been pacifying my needs. All she can do is hold me and keep saying you're not there. She cries with me, she holds me, she comforts me. There is nothing anyone can do except offer support for me when I'm there and not here. I am letting her in and dropping the walls of mistrust, and it is starting to feel pretty good.

DAY 23, 23OCT2007

Group was rough today. I talked about the first soldier to get his head chopped off by Al-Zaquari. I guess about 6 months ago, my battle buddy showed the clip to the Privates (PVTS). I was livid with anger. Since that moment, all the emotions and flashbacks started hitting harder than before. What my battle buddy didn't know was we sent several units, including mine, on several raids. We captured and killed more than 500 insurgents, but Al-Zaquari was always one step ahead of our Intel. We always missed him by 5-10 minutes. When they said the soldier was dead, my unit as well as the Army as a whole wept for him. No man deserves to die like that.

Then we talked about how in war we can manage almost any situation, but here at home it is very difficult to do. Don't get me wrong – war is controlled chaos, but here at home the line between black and white is clearly marked. Their grey areas persist.

Turning off the switch is hard for trained killers who are taught to disconnect with our reality to accomplish any mission. It always goes back to, men are human, and if they wanted machines to fight our wars, they should have made them.

Acceptance of this reality is a must in order for us afflicted with this to start to piece together the good of what we did instead of focusing on the losing end of the battles.

Are we in Baghdad for all the wrong reasons? Yes, we are. But my brothers and I didn't fight for US policy, because we all   know what that is; we fought for each other. Toward the end of my tour, all I was concerned about was getting out alive and getting my men out alive. There were no more politics on the streets of Baghdad; there was just survival. We didn't build schools, we didn't try to make a better social structure; we just fought to stay alive.

It still amazes me how we could do that type of work day in and day out with very little sleep. In 2004 we lost 1 American soldier a day.

I listened to the President's speech about Unbar Province, but nothing was mentioned about the security of Baghdad. That is because Baghdad will never be secured. The upcoming elections show promise of relief. The other Veterans and I who have seen the blood on the ground know this is a losing battle. But how can we win the battles at home when our reality is still trigger on!

Take 10 deep breaths...

You're home

You're safe

You're loved!

DAY 24, 23 OCT2007

The incident with which I was charged was litigated today. Jen and everyone showed up to the proceedings with me. I got off relatively light, considering all the actions that I took to get me in trouble. This, once again, was the causation of my crimes.

The dreams, anxiety, and flashbacks were more than I could bear at the time. Enough evidence was presented for my commander to make an informed and difficult decision. He did what he was supposed to do, like I did what I was supposed to do over in the desert.

When it all comes down to it, we all have suffered tremendously because of my actions that have been haunting me in the past and currently.

I am very happy that Jen has stood by me through all of this trouble I brought to the Army. I have fallen. I have felt betrayed, and I have felt lost in the machine. Now the only answer is to stand up. Stand up and fight for the soldiers who have no voice. Stand up and tell all the others who are scared to speak that I will speak for them. Tell others that they are not alone. Tell them I know what the pain feels like. I know what it is like to feel alone, lost and that no one cares. And finally, I truly know what it means to finally say:

"GET BUSY LIVING OR GET BUSY DYING!

FIND A PATH TO PEACE!"

TWO WEEKS LATER, 4 NOV2007

Well, a lot has happened since my Article 15 hearing. I continue to do my duty, although very mundane at times. Working in the S-3 shop in a basic training unit consists of a lot of BS. I hate it there; there is nothing for me to do. Every time I walk into that office I feel failure written all over me.

I saw the medication doctor. She's keeping me on Zoloft plus sleep medicine. After years of trying, I finally got a full night's sleep. Not just one night, either, but several nights. Jen, once again, is supportive. I take the medicine at 8:30, so by 9:30 or so I am knocked out.

I've been having some serious breakthroughs the last couple of weeks. Finally, in group I confessed why I was so angry. My men and I had a total of 35 engagements with the enemy. These men showed valor beyond anything I could have imagined! They were calm under pressure and made battlefield decisions for me. I listened to them. Even though I was senior to them, they were all my brothers. What did all of us get for finding over 100 IEDs, surviving a car bomb hitting our back deck, car bombs, snipers, rockets, air bursting mortars? Well, the answer is an Army Commendation Medal (Arcom). It was truly a slap in the face. I tried to put all of them in for bronze stars, but it all got denied. However, if you were a Sergeant First Class (SFC) or Lieutenant (LT), you got a bronze star. There is no doubt my LT deserved his, but my next LT that joined us 7 months into the tour even got one. That has been hard to swallow.

I remember all the awards ceremonies when we got back. Jen pinned my 5th Arcom on my chest, and then her and I walked through and pinned the awards on the guys. We all stood there, numb and disgusted, and when it was over there were Arcom's lying around on the ground. I went straight to my car, ripped it off my chest and threw it in my glove box. It's still there to this day. Jen knew all about it. She didn't say a word; she was just so happy I was home safe.

I kept on thinking during the whole thing that rank has its perks. My other friend whom I served with was a Platoon SGT as an SSG, and the next promotion he was selected to SFC. He told me it was all because of the bronze star! I agreed, congratulated him, and walked away seeing my career going straight down the toilet.

A lot of people say you can get a Combat Infantry Badge for just being in country. That is true, but my 2 CIBs I earned. I didn't want the Purple Heart, but I got one. We did things that should be recognized as true valor, but they didn't recognize our accomplishments. One of the triggers for this disease is lack of trust in the chain of command. How can I trust an army that tries to save money at every turn? I mean, let's get real here - how much could it really cost to have 24 bronze stars made?! Their explanation for the lack of acknowledgement was we didn't do anything spectacular; we just did our jobs. Well, in my opinion, anybody who is there outside the wire deserves the recognition of this nation and top honors. That is why the Arcom's were lying on the ground. I challenge any reader of this hell I'm going through to tell me I'm wrong on that point.

Bitterness has consumed my soul along with anger, depression, and an inability to feel sympathy. No wonder I'm so jacked up.

People always say you can't change what's not broken; let's see…so far by my calculations 30,000 of us feel the same way. Then what is Bush's war machine going to do? A lack of faith in the government and the mission is why we're losing in Baghdad. Try to sugar coat it all you want. We are losing that fight! Does that mean that the men I know did it for nothing? No, it doesn't. They did it for the brothers beside them and for a country that is starting to forget why we're fighting in the first place.

DAY 48, 5 NOV2007

Today seemed to be the roughest yet. After surviving group, I met up with Jen and went to a marriage retreat class. During that class Battalion called me to finish signing the proposal to remove me from the DS program.

At my Article 15 reading, I signed away my rights to appeal the adjudication. This was the hardest thing I ever did. I did not consult with Jen on that, because what was the use?

Since I had been hospitalized, I realized that Jen and the boys are the only things I have left. Throughout my career, I've seen guys try to fight the system and get destroyed. I have already lost my soul, which I'm trying to get back. Why would I risk everything when they let me off light?

I do have another outlet now. Jen and I are convicted to seeing this new manual made. I couldn't fight the crime, but I can fight for those still lost. I feel lost any way I go. Jen says I should have fought, that the PTSD was out of control. Unfortunately, it's not that easy.

For the first time, I put the welfare of my family first. I thought about them and how much a court martial would have destroyed us, and how a higher appeal has the possibility of my losing all of my rank, restriction, and the thing that hurts the most, money. With four kids to feed, what was I supposed to do? Even if I took counsel from Jen, I probably would have signed.

But this fight isn't done yet. I won't go away quietly into the night. I won't just retire and be satisfied. I won't leave the Army like this. I'll leave with my head high.

The pain of my crime and betrayal to the corps, plus my lying and covering up all that I did all these years to Jen, have given me enough pain. Baghdad keeps my soul, and now the Army took all that I kept in my heart that was good away too.

How much more can I take? How much more can my 17-year marriage take? Trust is so hard when you haven't trusted anyone your entire life; a very sad, depressing life. I am unable to truly feel Jen. On some things it is just easy to think by myself. I do know this: I have decided that I'm finally done with the Army, and that I truly do love my wife and kids. The Army says they support families in tough times, but it's all just lip service for a majority of soldiers searching for the peace in their hearts and minds.

All of us are perceived as weak, pusses, because the machine doesn't break. Well, I got news for them. People break, people feel. I've been a good suck-it-up type of guy for 18 years. **NOT ANY MORE!!!!!!**

DAY 49, 7NOV2007

Yesterday's group was extremely difficult for me. I kept on seeing my gunner's head split from the top of his brow down to his nose.

My depression is worsening now. I feel back to not wanting to move at all. I'm exhausted again and unable to be productive in my job.

I met with my therapist yesterday, and she tried to explain to me that I had these sexual urges before I joined the Army. She said I dissociate with the feeling of love and sex because of what my adopted mother had done to me and my brother. I can still remember standing in the kitchen of the old house in Kansas City, Kansas, naked and crying as Sonja pulled our penises and slapped our scrotums until we could not feel anything else. She told us to get up when the blows from her slaps knocked us to the ground. The kitchen floor was brown tile, and the living room was a horrible baby blue. Ironic that the color I hate worst in the world is on my right shoulder. I hated that house. I can remember every detail. My first experience with sex was a magazine rack filled with pornography in my father's room. No hiding it, just right out in the open. I saw in those magazines what I thought love was: Women in explicit positions, bodily fluids all over their faces and various other parts of their bodies; men sleeping with men, women with women. There was absolutely no trying to hide all that material. Even to this day, my father has a locked and hidden-away locker filled with pornography.

Now to be fair to my father, he wasn't a very religious man at the time, and his marriage to Sonja was shaky at best. I still respect the man who saved me and my brother from the streets; however, that is about as far as it goes. He always told me that he couldn't be the type of father and grandpa that his dad was. It perplexes him to no end that I just couldn't accept his reasoning behind it.

I confronted him only once about what happened to me and Chip. He looked at me and said, "Why didn't you tell me?" I looked back and said, "Because I was 5." Like a 5-year-old would know to tell his father what was happening when he was away. Still, even though my statement as a man myself, who had been married for 5 years with sons of my own, was staggering to him, it gave no relief of pain for me. His total lack of acknowledgement about my whole life drives me crazy.

Finally, after joining the Army and getting a degree, I'm back to feeling like that scared kid in the kitchen, waiting for the hammer to fall. I have never had faith in myself, even less for others. The Army was a good system for me. They don't want soldiers to feel. If they do feel, they are ostracized for their emotions.

I cut my side of the family loose. After all these years, I wanted my father's approval, acceptance, and understanding. That will never happen. I knew he truly didn't know how I felt when I asked him to watch my nephews for 2 weeks when I got back from Baghdad. He said no, that I was not the only soldier who has been to war or gotten wounded. From that point on I let him go. If he wants to be a part of my family, then he knows my number. He has never called, and it's been about 2-1/2 years. Kind of like I dropped off the planet.

This feeling of pure rejection is why I joined to begin with; however, I have never had the self-esteem to go further than I could have. Finally I can say I am finally done. I am so tired.

DAY 49, 8NOV2007

See the doctor – the feeling is back!

Yesterday I was feeling worse than I ever had, even before the Article 15, even before I committed the crime. I thought I was doing well. I was communicating, I was sharing, I went to all my combat groups. I have done everything I'm supposed to do, and yet yesterday morning I thought about my combat knife I had in the war and slicing my own throat. The wrist thing is too slow; but not over the major artery on the inside of my thigh. I picked that artery because I've seen a lot of wounded soldiers get hit in the leg and bleed out within a minute.

Why would I feel worse after working so hard? I tried everything, having a safe place, not withdrawing, trying to control all the flashbacks...I just don't understand.

So, I'm in a new hospital with some old friends. James is here, a soldier from the last hospital. My first day is about to begin, so I'll finish later with today's entry.

The kid's psych ward is right next to ours. This morning a kid was out of control and pounded on the holding room door. I instantly flashed back to the minivan with all the dead kids and a woman screaming as I was trying to load up all the wounded in my track. I actually told one guy who was interviewing me to shut the kids up and keep loading the wounded. He was staggered by that proclamation and ran and got some of the staff to help me. They separated me and calmed me down.

While I was in the middle of many interviews for the morning, I called Jen and thanked her for taking me to the doctor again yesterday. She said she loved me and just wanted me to get better. I thought I was doing good, but I guess with all that had happened lately the boiling point had been reached. I keep on struggling with the fact that my career is just about over. This will probably be it for me, depending on how long this stay is. They'll probably chapter me under a mental health discharge. That would be great on my record. I am truly a boat getting tossed on a rolling, turbulent sea. More to follow…

On the TV right now are rock videos, and it reminds me about how right now I really miss my music. Jen got me an iPod Nano for my 36th birthday. Over there we would all gather in a circle before the missions and play "Let the Bodies Hit the Floor," some G&R and Metallica just to get pumped up. Then after the missions there was a total shift of mood like Barry Manilow, Pavarotti, Neil Diamond, all the rock ballads. I always thought it humorous for big, tough infantrymen after a mission to be listening to jazz, opera, and classical music. Music was our release there. We didn't have enough time for anything else. I remember getting so mad at my gunner for having his headphones on during mission, but now I truly understand. I know that he could only focus when he separated himself from battle.

DAY 50, 9NOV2007

Last night I couldn't sleep again. I was all wound up about the conversation Jen and I had. She found out that they are trying to push through my Relief of Cause without my signature. I knew that they would try that crap. When I am hospitalized, they always try to be slick and kick me when I'm down.

I am very upset at the Unit because of this whole deal, but I'm just a whiner and complainer, even though I have 5 Arcom's, 15 Army Achievement Medals, a college degree, and numerous other awards. People fear what they don't understand.

Last night I rolled my sheet up and made a slipknot in it, wide enough to put my head through. I took it into the bathroom, just to find out there's nothing to hang myself with. So I let this book carry my pain. Let this book bear the weight of all my emotions.

When you're this low, I don't think you can get any lower.

The Army is starting to spin my illness into something I had before I joined; just like them to try to screw the soldier out of more retirement with disabilities.

I didn't ask to go to war all these times, and I didn't ask to get this label around my neck. What I always asked out of the military was someone to actually care about my emotions, my feelings as a soldier. Jen was right; I want acknowledgement. That, however, will never come. So once again, I feel lost. Trying to say this was a preexisting condition is simply abuse.

CASH

In February 1991, the 100-Hour War was going on, and we stopped for a quick re-supply post below a place called Objective (Obj) Bear. It was actually called something lasting. All I remember was it was pretty hairy there, and Obj Bear was a massive objective. Then it was our turn. The scouts from 2-7Inf 3ID (MECH) would try to find a breach point when the tanks would move forward. The Iraqi defense was intense, and for a moment we were stopped. The tanks breached and the scouts found a breach on the left side, but Cash's Bradley got stuck in the breach. Before we launched, I had coffee with him that morning. They sent my platoon, 1st Platoon A-Co 1/7Inf, to go to the left to get him. When we arrived, the trench line was shooting at us from all angles. I saw a tank round streak across the sky and hit a tank on top of the Iraqi ammo point. It went up like a sunspot or flare on the ground.

Then the tanks turned their fire on us. Everybody was shooting at everybody. Anything that moved got shot, but with 3 elements attacking on all sides, friendly fire is inevitable. There is a guy in my PTSD group who said my unit was on the receiving end of hell. I have to agree with him. Super-sabot rounds were flying all over the place. One hit its mark right in the back of Cash's track. The Army said it was an RPG, but I can tell you no one identified anything, and from seeing and feeling an RPG hit I can guarantee that was no RPG.

The impact area and exit of the round darned near cut Cash in half. An RPG does not exit the vehicle. Cash died that day, and we couldn't get to him. We did manage to save the gunner and BC. That was the only loss we had, and it was friendly fire. He was my friend. I partied with him and we enjoyed each other's company, and now he was gone.

I walked up. I'll never forget the picture of his boots and rifle with his helmet in the sand. I gave Cash the slow salute and then walked away. When I got back from the war I drank heavily, then married Jen. The incredible thing about it was my PTSD symptoms started after watching Cash die. Even though it was a 100-hour war, it totally devastated some of us in the Unit.

My guilt also comes because I froze in combat. An SPC slapped me out of it, and I continued. Several men got wounded because of that. That is something I will never be able to let go. I was so young, so scared.

I stayed in the Army because I vowed to help others in combat, and I knew that we would be there again. Thirteen years later, I'm leading men in Baghdad. Ironic to this life of a true grunt.

ANGER IS BAD!!

DAY 52, 11NOV2007

Yesterday I celebrated my 36th birthday locked down in the ward. This other patient who is definitely mentally ill made me have to take a Valium. I slept on the couch in the day room on watch. I decided to teach the psych class. Hell, because I'm a criminology major it all fit together. The social workers said I was right on the money with my guilt class.

The whole time I was teaching, this fella kept pointing at me with a trigger finger snapping it back and laughing. He had a look in his eyes I had seen before: The dead stare of no emotion, and yet he continued to torment me. The look a bad guy has before he attacks. I've seen it a hundred times. He was smaller than me, an easy kill if I wanted to. My emotions started to kick in to a strictly defensive mode. I wasn't in the room anymore. I kept running scenarios in my head: Arm bar, choke out, behind the ear with my pin. I couldn't shut it off. I asked him if he was okay, but he didn't say anything. I said, "If you do the trigger thing again, you're dead." He left the room; I guess he saw in my eyes as well. That is the feeling I hate the most, knowing that I could have killed that guy in less than a minute. I feel out of control with my emotions here. I guess it's because of the treatments and the drugs.

Today is visiting day. I can't wait to see Jen and the boys.

Jen and the boys came to visit. I was still in a melancholy mood, and I believe Jen could feel it. She is convinced that once I start to heal I will want to stay in the Army. The truth is I would stay, but I'm Infantry and there is the war still going on. If I go back to war I would be ineffective, and they don't need a broken sergeant leading men in Baghdad. The visit was good.

THANK YOU JEN!!!

DAY 53, 12NOV2007

Last night was hell. Every time my door opened, I jumped out of my bed. The tech checked on us once an hour, standard practice for a mental hospital. There is a medic here, and boy, does he have some stories. I loved my medic. The line medics are the best this nation has to give.

My medic got 2 Purple Hearts. I tried to give him a bronze star, but as previously stated, that didn't go. Towards the end of my tour, 2 days before we were slated to leave sector, Doc got hit with the same sniper that shot at us all week. The bullet ripped through his back under his bullet-proof plates.

We were standing over him, twice now, asking him, "What do we do? Tell us what to do!" Doc kept telling us what to do as we loaded him in the back of the track.

The feeling of loss is even greater when your medic gets hit. The medic is the calming voice on the battlefield. He is the person to save and heal quickly. When he falls, it is felt throughout the platoon. I cried when Doc was hit. Not only did he patch up 16 of us under fire, but he was also a good friend. Even though he was a lower rank, he was and always will be our Doc.

The rest of the day has gone as usual. I almost got in a fight today with the mentally ill guy. I had to leave the group again. That is okay; I realize he has his demons too.

Some of the other Vets and I were talking about blending back into society today. I think that would be difficult for me because I am true Army. Many folks might read these passages some day and wonder if I do hate the army. The answer is no, I love the job; just mentally sometimes I break. I'm older now and starting to get my feelings back, and learning how to feel again is very difficult when you shut off the switch. Feelings hurt. I hate to say it, but it hurts to feel good.

Soul Catcher

I give these words to you, my book.

My heart has found no peace.

In this prose I rest easy,

Knowing that my soul is at ease.

With the knowledge of my eyes

And to feel the hurt in my face,

Brings me one step closer to you,

The silent lines of my soul catcher.

One step closer to finally finishing the race.

Divine is your blank page.

Easiness falls onto thee, my catcher, my soul, my book.

Patrol Prayer

God, protect me and my men on tonight's patrol. Give us strength and courage in our hour of need. Forgive me of all my sins, for I am unworthy of your grace. Give my enemy a quick and painless death, and bless my wife and kids so that I may live to see them again. Amen.

DAY 54, 3NOV2007

The prayer on the previous page I said every time I rolled out the gate. Kind of an odd quandary, that I would pray every day and yet I'm not a practicing Lutheran. I remember my step-mom telling me once that "I'm not raising my children to be Christians." I scoffed at that idea. Isn't the whole point of faith to believe in something that isn't there? I raise my kids to uphold all the commandments, even though I don't tell them verbally word for word. I do believe God was with me in Baghdad; otherwise, I would not be here.

I think the reason why we don't practice by going to church is because I see so many hypocrites in the church environment. Although men will be sinners, the whole goal is to try to achieve the greatness of God. I don't believe God to be as elusive as everyone thinks. What I do believe is that God is not very merciful; however, God gives mercy to those who need it. In this war, I've seen things that either make you turn away or come closer to God. God to me is an entity of immense power, and you don't have to ask much in order to receive a lot.

Throughout my life, I've been to churches of all kinds. Feeling of a spirit is a personal thing to me. Sure, there are those who say unless you profess your faith we are lost. I can quote you any passage you want. Since Wanda (step-mom) came into our lives, it was always fire and brimstone. There was no such thing as straddling the fence.

Which leads me to the reason why I'm writing so early in the day. Wanda met Mike (adopted dad) while he was divorcing Sonja (adopted mom). Sonja was a _(diabetic?)_ on the worst side. Even though Sonja did abuse us, it was clear what that type of abuse was. It was direct and single; we always knew where we stood with her. She had a monkey on her back; but with Wanda, the abuse was much more horrific in my eyes.

Divorce is ugly. Even though Sonja abused us, when the divorce came, my brother and I thought it was our fault. My father had to know about things that went on, because the visitation was minimal.

Not very long after the divorce, Wanda moved in. Dad was cool about it at first. We called her Wanda, and she respected that. I feel to this day that she was not prepared to come into marriage where two 10-year-old boys were already set on the path.

As soon as she married Mike, it was a total switch. We were forced to call her Mom. Very difficult for me to do. We were forced to do chores, forced to get good grades, just basically a whole paradigm shift. This transition was very difficult to accomplish for me because deep down, and it is still evident to this day, that she did not want leftover kids. To be fair, I probably wouldn't have, either. A couple of years later she had Heather, and Heather was really their first child in their relationship. That little girl changed the whole perspective of the father-son, mother-son relationship. Right away, my brother and I knew exactly that the little attention we got was now gone. Thus began the mental abuse.

Ignoring children is just as bad as not even having them. Mike and Wanda could go about their days, not having to worry about household chores, because my brother and I did them all. Mike was never a warm father. Many years later I found out he tried to give us back, but my grandma stopped him. So it has always, and will continue to, hit me that really no one except for my grandma and grandpa wanted us. My father and Wanda always asked, "Why were your grandparents so important to you?" He asked that again a couple of years ago, and my answer was they had unconditional love for us; Mike and Wanda's love was conditional. Always.

Fast forward to now. I adopted my nephews because my brother had no one else, and we never leave anyone behind. He begged my parents to let him back, but they ignored his plight. They were going to put the kids into a system that I know for sure is broken, so Jen and I took on the task ourselves. I have 2 sisters, Heather and Amanda. Heather is the oldest with Amanda close behind. When Heather got divorced from my team leader from Korea, who also was in the war with me, my parents allowed her to stay there with her kids for almost a year. Even though my brother is extremely manipulative, they had no thoughts of ever saving him or their 2 grandsons.

This has been a major blow to me and my brother, but not a blow that we didn't see coming. Our whole life with this family has been one of pure emotional neglect. I never braced myself for that but always knew it was there.

When I got home from the war, I pretty much told Wanda and Mike that if they wanted to be a part of my family let me know, and then I cut the umbilical cord. That was 2-1/2 years ago, and they still haven't called. My sister's living with them really put a deep bitterness in my heart, and yet they feel the same way I do. When you have no one, what are you supposed to do? They

(Mike and Wanda) think they're right and will never admit the wrongness of their actions, self-centered hypocrites who still go to church 3 times a week. That's not very Christian-like, is it?

Still the faith has not left me, because I wouldn't be here today if he weren't with me. So, once again that leaves me to ponder about the preexisting condition which I am afflicted with today. The answer is no! Mike had me for 14 years, and Wanda had us for about 8 years until I joined the Army. In those 8 years I never, ever once felt her love. When I was away from the house in my adult years, I tried to find that piece of my heart that was missing, and I never found it until I met Jen. Do the memories of cutting off the man who saved us from the streets hurt? Yes, they do; however, that pain is miniscule to the events that unfolded after I joined the Army.   I remember when I got wounded, the first person I called was my wife, and then I called Wanda. That same week she asked my wife why I called her and poured out my heart over the phone. My wife was staggered at that comment. I, on the other hand, was shocked but not disappointed, because I know she never wanted us. She has her own kids, and that's all she wanted. What kind of mother (a person I was forced to call Mom) wouldn't understand a son just wounded in combat trying to reach out for comfort?

Jen has been the only woman I could ever trust or love. That is not a preexisting condition. I cut them loose. My real mom is dead, my parents Mike and Wanda have not attempted to be close to me, so where is the loss? I'll tell you, Sonja is dead as well. The only family I had was Jen, the boys, and the Army. THANK YOU JEN, WITH ALL MY HEART!!!

DAY 55, 14NOV2007

Right now it is late at night here in the hospital. They gave me sleeping pills plus a bucketful of other medications.

I think at night about when we first arrived in Baghdad, we weren't really assigned anywhere, so we slept on the desert floor in an old, dilapidated bath house. Sleep is the optimal term here. Our patrol routes were simple: Launch 2 Bradley's from ECP (Entry Control Point) 7, go up and down Tampa, onto Michigan, and clear for convoys coming in.

Well, day 1 on checkpoint 39, our boys were set up to guard a bridge. This bridge was the last bridge heading north to Fallujah. We set up our security and sent out foot patrols to stop insurgents from bypassing storm ditches filled with 4 feet of water from getting by.

The fire team was in the middle of the clover leaf when a white car charged them. They raised their weapons to shoot, but it was too late. Five 155 rounds sent shockwaves through the air. One of my soldiers flew 150 feet to the other side of the waddie, and in a tenth of a second 15 of them were going home. Luckily none of them died, but many of them will not serve again.

The very next day another car bomb, same CP, put 2 more in the hospital. Later at CP-42 Michigan near the market, they lit off an ambush with RPGs. I saw the rocket hit the left front of the deck, then another. I yelled, "Action left!" and the follow-up Bradley hit the house. Now it's time to fight on foot and get those guys. I ordered white one towards   the back and do his drop there; he did. I was going to drop cattycorner to the building; my drop was perfect. They entered . As I was raising my ramp, a 200-pound car bomb drove right into the back of us, bowing the Bradley ramp out so we couldn't close it. We were dead, I thought, until all of us came to 3 minutes later. We MedEvac'd 3 of our guys out on that one.

I was getting so tired of getting hit and then they run. They like to think they're fighting honorably, but there is no honor in an asymmetrical war that has no winners. America wonders why we are knocking ourselves off: Because we can't live with the pain of failure. We are called the greatest generation; we thought we learned from Vietnam. Well, America, we haven't. We want the bleeding to stop!

DAY 56, 15NOV2007

Today I can't stop shaking. My hands and legs are constantly shaking. This is a distressing feeling. To be able to shoot you have to have a steady hand. To be able to fight you must be steady, be able to think clearly, assess the situation. I've noticed since my return that my hands are unsteady and my short-term memory is gone. I find it difficult to even remember where I laid the car keys after putting them down 5 minutes ago. This is not anything that has happened before. I prided myself as being very sharp, an edge-of-the-blade person and the effectiveness to kill.

Now I have unsteady thoughts, trembling extremities that are difficult to control. Constantly my muscles twitch and tremor against my will. Even Jen has noticed that my muscle control has become strained.

I know there is something wrong with my head. I faint for no reason every now and then. I see things in black and white all the time. Something is wrong, I know it is. I'm exhausted today, and if I don't sleep my body shakes worse. The doctors haven't said anything, yet I have an MRI scheduled to try to find out what is wrong with me neurologically.

Right now I think I'm in the middle of a panic attack. I can feel my heart pounding out of my chest. It is difficult to get a breath. I first have to breathe, not withdraw. Absorb the pain and relax all of my muscles. I wish I had my music!

DAY 57, 16NOV2007

Had nightmares last night, usual ones at best. The nightmare itself, though, was very unusual. I was at the hospital and I couldn't stop having orgasms, but the semen that came out was like a green-blue color. It hurt me so bad, but the doctors didn't know what to do and they couldn't stop it.

I don't think I'm ready for Dominic's group. We talk about a lot of issues. He is a good psychologist. He doesn't let anyone off the hook.

My anger today was out of control. I had to be sedated, and I told the staff not to get close to me.

My anger stems from how badly the Army is treating us with this syndrome. Their total lack of acknowledgement is really starting to get to me.

Jen read me an article from <u>The Turret</u>, which is the post newspaper, about how the Army family takes care of its own. I used to believe that, but now with the medical boards and all of the diagnoses, they're screwing us out of what is rightfully ours. Our benefits were paid in blood, and they're always going to try to get the lowest number they can. I am so disappointed in the military right now that it is unbelievable.

I remember the Vietnam Vets protesting; I wish I could myself.

DAY 58, 17NOV2007

Two Air Force officers are here in the hospital with me. One seems very open for conversation, while the other is closed off and treats us like NCOs. I guess I can't complain; I still am an NCO.

I've been thinking about Steve lately. Steve was one of my soldiers on a security mission in Kuwait, the Udari Range. Udari is the hottest place on the planet; 170 degrees in the shade, sandstorms every day. The heat is truly unbearable. We would go to Kuwait for 6-month rations as a security and backup QRF for Kuwaiti forces. While we were there we trained in the heat. This was way before the Army started giving us AC in the tents.

One mission we went on to practice was to breach a portion of an objective. Steve was the OpFor (opposing force) on a little sand dune. Steven and I were friends right away because he hailed from Minneapolis, Kansas, and I'm from KC. Anyway, the sandstorm was extremely brutal that day. Some storms you can't even see 2 feet in front of you. Imagine standing in a giant oven with someone sandblasting your whole body. That's Udari.

Steve was the spotter for an AT-4 gunner that was supposed to blast the flanking Bradley's. The fight was on, and we quickly started to flank. Steve told the gunner to hold fire, he was shifting positions. Well, the sand and wind blocked the gunner's hearing and he pulled the trigger. The back-blast of the inert round was 40 feet. It hit Steve square   in the chest. Over 1000 degrees of fire engulfed him. His desert battle uniform was burned into his skin all the way to the small of his back. He put up his hands, and the gloves he was wearing melted to his hands. Third-degree burns covered his whole upper body, and he swallowed some of the flame, burning his throat. We heard over the net Steve was down. We rushed to his side. I knelt down, and I saw a horrible sight. The guy who pulled the trigger tried to take off his gloves, and in doing so ripped the flesh right off his hands. Steve couldn't breathe. I immediately put a J-tube down his throat and did my best to keep him calm. The medics arrived. I got on the track with him whispering, "You're not going to die here!"

The doctors worked quickly, and there the Big Green Foot (Air Force Jolly Green Giant medical chopper) came and got him. I walked with him all the way to the LZ. The chopper lifted off, and I thought he would make it.

I can still see his arm muscles hanging there like fresh roast beef and his screaming. Later on that week, someone told me that he had died at the hospital. That crushed me, and I wept for my soldier.

But when I got home, he walked up to me as I got off the bus and said, "SGT Freeman, I'm alive, thanks to you. You saved my life." I wept again, but happy tears. Now Steve is a sheriff in his home town of Minneapolis, Kansas.

> I always save lives but find it
> hard to save my own!

DAY 58-59, 17-18OCT2007

Yesterday was rough. A new guy arrived to the hospital. Among the military guys on break, he jumped into the conversation. He started bragging about how much he travels to Afghanistan to buy opium plants. He arrived with opium on him. It automatically made me think of Doug. Doug died in Afghanistan. I got so angry at his comments that I had to separate myself from the group. My anger was beyond anything that I have felt in treatment before.

We gave our blood in Afghanistan so this guy could take the drug-selling profits that the Taliban uses to support their terrorist activities. I really wanted to kill that guy.

Last night they started me on a new sleep medication. I've noticed that with the sleep medication my nightmares come more frequently. I think that it is truly because I have suppressed all of the pain from my career in the back of my mind. Hiding deep in my head lays the pain of all my combat tours. I've also noticed that I tend to talk a lot more in my sleep, bringing out all of my hidden secrets. When Jen started to help me in this process in the hospital, she mentioned that my sleep was very disturbed. In an odd way, it could be one of the reasons I didn't sleep, strictly because of that. The pain in my head that has been put to the side along with my insomnia was too afflicting to me. So sleep is something I haven't gotten in 3 years.

Once again, I have another battle to fill my long recovery. That is to fully know that my sleep also has its demons.

DAY 60-61, 19-20OCT2007

For 2 nights now I've slept okay. I was talking about my Purple Heart, and that kind of brought back a flashback of that day. I'm not ready to write about that yet.

This evening they started my neurologic testing, and it started me to be triggered. Thank God it's in phases. I get my MRI on Friday, and I'm extremely nervous. A brother came back to the ward today, crying. I asked Dave what was wrong. He said he got his results back. He said that his results are starting to show dementia. He had a lot of explosions, too. I was upset, he was upset…hell, what a great day.

The amount of pain in this place is indescribable. These brothers in here are getting ignored, just like I was. The Army should have recognized all this stuff a lot earlier. My rage because of all this is just unbearable. It doesn't matter; why should the machine start for me or stop? I just have to get used to it.

DAY 60, 22NOV2007

I am in a melancholy mood today. Yesterday was a good day. Also, today was my son's birthday. He is growing up, and yet I still feel as if he is my little boy. I know for sure he feels as if sometimes I don't love him. For half of Tyler's life I haven't been there for his birthdays, and yet once again I am not there for his birthday. I do love my son, and I think deep down he does believe I love him. He is truly his father's son. He does know why I am here. That brings me comfort on some of my weakest days.

Today is Thanksgiving. I do have a lot to be thankful for. Just to be alive is the best thing for me right now, and seeing the whole family is a blessing.

DAY 61, 23NOV2007

I went to get my MRI today. I hope it can shed some light on what is going on in my head. The Unit told Jen that I am a soldier and will be taken care of by soldiers. What audacity this Unit has! I tried to be nice. I haven't gotten angry about a lot of things; however, not letting Jen be involved in my recovery is ridiculous. The nerve of this Unit's NCO corps!

I am glad I'm hanging up my hat in this Unit. I knew they were trying to be secretive about what was going on the whole time. Jen didn't do anything to this Unit, and for someone to say she is not a part of my recovery is going beyond their purpose of leadership.

At this point, I'm so fed up with the Army that I can't even say how disappointed I am about how they have left me behind, and now they are starting to leave my family behind. That is unacceptable. For that, they will suffer as soon as I get back. I will confront the chain of command. I don't care what they think; I really don't care what they try to do to me. Someone has to step up; this has gone on long enough.

On top of all this drama, I had nightmares all night long. No matter what happened, I could not get away from the enemy's mortar attacks. I woke up screaming at the top of my lungs, covered in sweat. It scared me so much I couldn't get back to sleep. They're coming back for some reason. I don't know how to control my anxiety in my sleep. It's not like I can control those. How do I control my dreams? Just another battle to fight.

DAY 62, 24NOV2007

I have made lifelong friends here and some business opportunities. It would seem that my gift of gab is in need throughout this area, and I've been hired by 2 men to be their personal _(trainers?)_. I wish and pray that this goes a long, long way. I've never thought of myself as a motivational speaker before. As I look back on my military career, I think about how I motivated my men to do the wrong thing the right way.

I do have the gift to talk to people and tell them what they want to hear. Some folks might call that arrogance, but I call it a skill. So many men and women find comfort in my words. Now I pray that I can share all of that with the world. I can do this. I am important to my family, and Jen believes in me. Finally, after 61 days, I am starting to believe in myself.

DAY 65, 27NOV2007

I'm finally ready to tell my wounded story. It was near checkpoint 34, just down the road from the prison in Abu-Graib. We were continuously hit at that checkpoint. The enemy would mortar us from the marine sector. The marine sector was to the west of us. Literally, if you walked west 10 feet, you were in the marine sector.

I came up with a plan to do a counter-ambush recon through their sector. The marines were busy with Fallujah and hadn't been in their sector for 6 months. All of that information, however, was unknown to me at the time. All I knew was I was tired of getting hit. We lost 6 men at that checkpoint, and by God, we weren't going to lose anymore.

I convinced my LT to take up the counter-ambush patrol. I figured that if the enemy was scared out they wouldn't hit the checkpoint. I decided to do this being the senior NCO on the ground. He went for it, and we launched our vehicles. Throughout my tours in Baghdad, I was lead point for over 200 patrols. I was stupid in my underestimation of the enemy's conviction.

There was a 4-way corner with some hajji shops. These are shops that are pretty much thrown together with wood and string. A good stiff wind would blow it over, and for the life of me I can't remember the little town on the edge of the sector that all the leathernecks hadn't been to in a long, long time.

I do remember clearly that 4-way intersection accompanying the town. That was the first time I actually felt the pure hate the Iraqi people had for us.

There were no kids running beside our patrol. No one waved. They just stood there with blank stares at us. Their eyes never even blinked as their black dowels looked at us. When you saw that, you knew you were in the right place. It had to be a sunflower seed farm, because all they had in this area was sunflower fields. It is not all desert in Baghdad.

That day we headed out and hit the route at the same time of day as the last 3 days. I was definitely concerned with our ability to hit the same areas of patrol route day after day. I knew that we should've kept the enemy guessing; a lesson I soon learned the hard way.

My gunner and I were riding high at this part of our tour (open hatches, standing up), blissfully unaware of any danger to ourselves. I had been in several ambushes before. My crew and I were almost arrogant in our confidence to sniff out an ambush, but today wasn't the day. We reached a stretch of road that was a perfect choke point for the bad guys. In the hedge rows and flowers, lying in wait in the creek beds, Hajji waited.

We arrived just in time. I thought one hedge row looked different, but before I could ask my gunner to scan it with the gun, all hell broke loose.

Two 155 artillery rounds laced together and went off to my left front. The blast threw shrapnel onto me and my gunner. He dropped automatically. My helmet and safety glasses were shattered and blown off my head as the initial shockwave of rock and metal hit me square in the chest.

The vehicle stalled, and my driver was knocked out in the kill zone. Anyone who has been to Infantry school knows being stuck in the kill zone is bad news.

Blood started to fill my left eye. I looked down at my gunner. A piece of metal was sticking out of his forehead and dark blood was pumping out in a stream. Every beat was a spurt. I froze for a split-second, trying to access the BDA (Battle Damage Assessment). I put my hand over my gunner's forehead and flipped some switches to try to get power back to my main gun.

Just then I heard the silent whisper of mortars coming in. I jumped on the radio and asked my wingman to engage the creek bed to our right. He did so and scared them out. My Infantry on foot laid down fire. At that time the LT was concerned about me and my gunner, and he made his way over to the track. I got the power back and engaged while having one hand on my gunner's head.

It was all over in less than 3 minutes. I know that seems short, but it lasted forever. Later on in the tour we would capture bad guys from the same cell we engaged.

I couldn't talk. The LT, while mortars were coming in, bandaged me and my gunner up. He switched personnel and got us out of there. My Bradley took significant damage to the left front (see picture).

When we arrived at the CSH (Combat Support Hospital, "cash"), the whole Brigade chain of command was there, wondering why this Lieutenant went into the marine sector. I took full credit for the decision that wounded 2 of us. As I learned the hard way, trying to make yourself an easy target works in Baghdad. The mission was called a "successful failure" in that we knew where to hunt now, but at the cost of one $150 million track and 2 wounded soldiers.

DAY 66, 28NOV2007

I had another moment of clarity today as I sat in Dominic's PTSD group. I realized that Jen is still around, so I can give back to her all of the love she has given me over the last 17 years. As I look back at this war, all my tours and as a drill instructor, Jen has been waiting patiently for me to love her like I love the Army. So, I am sitting there overwhelmed with emotion concerning that moment of clarity. A rush of pure love came over me as I finally understood what she had been talking about all those years.

Jen is a firm believer in not throwing in the towel when times got hard. I long for her touch even more these days. I set up my barriers because I didn't want to let her in to share my pain, and now that I have nothing more to hide from her, I find it easier to tell her the truth, to hold her, to kiss her, to pay attention to her, to be sensitive to her needs now and not my own selfish acts. This hospital and others like it help the solders and the family. I wished I wasn't so hard-headed all those years.

Since I have opened up to her, my pain is becoming more manageable and the experience of combat is starting to not be as difficult. Sure, I will always have nightmares, but now I truly feel blessed and loved by God and the only woman on this planet who had the courage to save me.

Now I can finally say with pride this is my wife Jen, the toughest, most competent, sound lover I have ever had, and the most wonderful battle buddy a solder could have. This is my wife Jen, whom I love dearly and have not forgotten!

DAY 67, 29NOV2007

My psych training is back today. They said there were significant findings of brain damage from getting socked so much in Baghdad. This is not a new finding to me and Jen. I know for a fact my short-term memory is gone. I literally have to write everything down in order to remember names, locations, and numbers.

Tomorrow Jen is coming by to get the full reading of the test. _(Genology)_ has not played a part in this, and I now have a confirmed diagnosis directly linking my behavior, my rage, sexual deviance, moods, and exhaustion. PTSD sufferers multiply these mood disorders ten-fold, according to the VA.

It has been determined that if I go back to the Infantry line, I would be a danger to myself and others. That is not a good thing. So now I know what I have to do: Fight to get my name cleared and fight to get my full 20 years. If they don't give me the full 20, I will get a lawyer and sue for the last 2 years of my career.

It does, however, seem that I would have to be resigned to a family-run business. I have already told TJ and Lu, and they're in. That is fine with me. Can I accomplish everything that my father didn't? The only reason I joined 18 years ago is because I had no hope and was told I had no hope of a future.

Well, I do have a future, and even though my military record was tarnished by a couple of disciplinary actions, there isn't a guy I have ever served with who said they wouldn't follow me anywhere on the planet. I do hate the war, but I love the Army. I have met great American brothers I was proud to share the shit with.

That is something my father never had. I'm successful, a good leader, and a hell of a father and husband. It is finally time to start giving myself credit for all I've done. I am a lucky man and love my family. The Army loved me in a firefight, so there is no greater victory in life than that.

I am Good enough.

I had a good

Career.

<u>My family loves me</u>.

Time to retire! I am ready to be me again!!

DAY 68, 1DEC2007 - The night we took our stand

I look back at all we have done over there and wonder if we could have done more. I remember saying the rollout prayer, then kneeling down and throwing up. One night we knew we were going back into hell, so I gave the men a speech before we left.

I gathered all the men around me. The LT did his thing, then looked at me and asked, "SGT, you have anything to add?" I told them, "We've been hit every time we go down that road. Tonight we make our stand! We'll leave 1 Bradley in over watch, checking rooftops and calling in sit-reps to the LT and the Infantry on the ground. My Bradley will provide blocking from enemy fire and be a bounding lead. If the LT gets hit, we'll bound forward with 2 tracks and block the enemy fire so the LT can flank the enemy's position. Shift fires and actions on the objective will be strictly controlled by the LT. I'll handle _(med-evact?)_ and air support."

So we launched, knowing we were going to get hit. At about the same time in the evening, 0200, the foot patrol launched down the street. I put my wingman in the support-by-fire position and stayed off the Infantry foot patrol by about 50 meters. They were using lighted flashlights, looking for IEDs. This technique was quickly and promptly stopped later in the tour, because too many men were dying. A bullet ricocheted by the LT's foot. They did their job, they got engaged. The fire started to get heavier as they sought covered positions, but they could not see where the fire was coming from. That was my job. We pushed forward, and with the thermals we saw them. A fire team (3-5 men) was bounding forward toward the LT. They were poorly trained, because they didn't support their bound. Anyway, the LT was pinned down. We pulled forward and waited until they were fully exposed. When they heard the track, 2 ran away, 2 stayed and engaged us, and 1 was running into a house. My gunner identified the 2 near the house. I gave the fire command. Instantly my Co-Ax (240B machine gun mounted) lit up the night sky and cut down the one lodging in the doorway. I shifted to his other buddy and let go with another burst. We hit him as he went over the wall. I stopped firing and checked to see if anyone was hurt. The body count was 1 dead bad guy, 1 wounded still in play.

Turns out these were the people who were hitting us every night, and it was a family affair. We identified the living wounded bad guy and the dead one as brothers. They would get paid $100 for every American they killed, plus bonuses. These people were Iraqi citizens trying to feed their family. This was a common theme as the war wore on.

Eventually, we fought at least every bad guy who had a grudge with the US. Baghdad was the melting pot of bad guys. There were old Soviet Block bad buys, Syrians, Palestinians, Saudis, Indians, and a hundred other nationalities that we fought. Hell, I remember one we looked for. We called him the Snowman, because he was white with white hair. He would stick out like a sore thumb. He was in sector to teach how to shoot. He was an old sniper from the old Soviet Union. We never did find that guy, but towards the end of the tour the snipers he trained would wound and kill 15 of our men.

This is what the American public isn't told. Baghdad will never be secured, because of all the nations that want to fight American soldiers filter in to Baghdad. Why wouldn't they? The underdeveloped nations that profit from criminal activity to keep their families fed can come to Baghdad and get paid for every American flag they get. The bad guys recruit with money and financial freedom. As long as they are allowed to recruit like that the war would continue, but that night in early September 2004 we made our stand and won one small battle for peace in Baghdad.

DAY 69, 2DEC2007

Today was visiting day here at the hospital. Jen brought all the boys except for one. Bradley is at another mental health hospital. Bradley is a key to my recovery, because he's my adopted son, previously my nephew.

My 2 nephews are the product of my mentally retarded brother and his staying-on-subsidies wife, Kelly. Jen and I had been trying to get the boys since they were born. The boys have pretty much been on their own since being born. I remember one time when I was in Korea, Jen went to their 1-room apartment and both boys were eating pizza boxes to stay alive. That same week the Kansas City, Kansas police found them playing naked under the 18th Street Expressway bridge.

Jen and I tried to use Social Services of Kansas before too much damage was done. The only form of discipline Bradley and Levi understood was direct violence. Jen and I speculate that Bradley had his jaw broken at least once as a child. The amount of abuse these boys went through is staggering to me, and I've been through a lot myself. The boys and Chip and Kelly for a long time lived with the in-laws. My side of the family wanted nothing to do with Chip or the boys (more on that later). Chip tried his best to feed the kids, but Kelly would eat all the food. At the in-law's house, Bradley got a steady beat-down. Once, he had his arm handcuffed to a dinner table for days. The kids would get put in a closet with no light or food for days. Kelly's idea of prison. Chip could not control his anger, so any stepping out of line was a belt and fist.

Jen and I knew all this abuse was going on, so we finally had the attention of the state. Both Chip and Kelly fled to Florida with the kids. They bounced around from hotel room to hotel room. Kelly would get a job as a housemaid in order to get lodging for weeks at a time. Meanwhile, the boys remained by themselves to get food. Bradley tells how he and his little brother would stand in front of McDonald's and beg for food. As a matter of fact, when we first got them they walked up to a person in a restaurant and asked for his food. I apologized to the person and then told the boys they would never have to worry about food ever again.

Food is a major issue with kids who have been diagnosed with separation anxiety. They were also diagnosed with ADD and social disorder. So as you can see, Jen and I had our hands full from the start.

I first met the older boys when Chip's wife left him in Florida to go live with a roofer in Louisiana. Chip knew he couldn't survive. The kids had no shoes, had soiled clothes and hadn't eaten in 3 days. He called my parents, and they called Jen. This was 2 weeks before I was scheduled to come home from Baghdad. I got off the plane, and there they were. I asked my parents to watch Chip and the boys while I went on my 30-day leave. Of course, they said no. That has been a serious point of contention with my oldest son Tyler, who just wanted his dad to love him and pay attention to him after a year of worrying about me. To this day, Tyler and Lucas (middle son) haven't talked to their grandparents since.

I had no choice but to take my brother and the boys in and take them on leave with me, as we traveled the Purple Heart trail to go say goodbye to some of the men I knew at Arlington. On top of all this, I was slated to go to DS school that winter. Needless to say, the trip was good but very brutal.

I hadn't come home yet from the war and was still very uneasy. Jen set up the trip at a 5-star resort with a golf course I could play on. The trip was great for me and Jen; however, spending all that money for my family and Chip's family was really bothering me the whole trip. Chip eventually would lose out, and after all I did for him, he would sign away his parental rights in the adoption. Kelly, the one who sexually and physically abused the boys, would be judged and forced to give up her parental rights as well. Then Jen and I paid for a divorce, once again to help my brother.

After 2-1/2 years of having the boys, the amount of stress from work and home finally got to me, as I mentally was going downhill. I finally gave up on Bradley and tried to cope. Bradley would urinate everywhere, jump out his window, crap on the floor, etc., and would only respond to a man's voice. So now he is in inpatient treatment across the street from me. I can't help Bradley unless I help myself first.

I pray every day that what is left of my soul will find mercy for those 2 boys and finally give Bradley peace. I told him tonight he was a good kid with a monkey on his back. As for my recovery, I can then help little Bradley and Levi to live a better life and be at peace.

Peace. What an odd word. I haven't felt it in 18 years, and it is elusive to me. Almost like praying to win the lottery and getting disappointed every time you lose.

I believe as Bradley and I share this journey to find peace that God will bless our family and finally grant us peace.

I have not yet given credit to God and understand him. Maybe I should humble myself before him and ask for peace in my mind. I do pray for my family, but I haven't prayed for myself in 18 years. Does that show lack of faith? Probably not; it shows that I humble myself to everyone else's wishes before my own.

I always told Jen that things would work out, that God has kept me alive through all of this for a reason. I don't know why God spared me all those times in the war, but it is truly time to start giving back and not be so ungrateful. I didn't die over there like so many of my friends. Maybe it is time to embrace my legacy and understand that I am not in control, to let go of my reins, and to praise him for keeping me alive! "Once more unto the breach, once more!"

> "Yea, though I walk through the valley of the shadow of death, I fear no evil. Thy rod and Thy staff, they comfort me. You have made me lie down in green pastures and have delivered me from evil.

> "What was made from the Earth shall return to the Earth. Ashes to ashes and dust to dust. Always in your name, Amen."

> It is time, my friends! Carpe Diem (seize the day)!!

DAY 70, 3DEC2007

It is time to get a hold of my anger. I'm very bitter about the war. I feel as if we haven't completed the task.

Americans by nature are winners, and to lose is the worst possible scenario that a soldier can face. There isn't a guy who has ever said we won in Baghdad. I am angry at that. I'm upset that the politicians don't know what is going on there. For 2-1/2 years, I've been simmering about the Iraq war. I fail almost every time I try to step back and take an objective view. There are a majority of Vets who feel the same way.

The pain of the war will always be with me. I took a destructive pattern to express this anger. I used sex as a crutch, and for that I am also angry. I am mad at my side of the family. I am angry at the Army. I am just plain angry!!

So, I guess the thing is now that I have finally been honest with myself, I will try to find coping skills that can reduce my anxiety. There is no answer for the war. As far as my family is concerned, I could try to confront them, but I doubt that would change things. Staying away from the Army is the best thing I could do right now.

I have 45 days of leave set up. I need to just get away and have some real family time. Real family time would be a good thing. I can't remember the last time I had some real family time.

DAY 71, 4DEC2007

Today, listening to the other soldiers in group made me so angry that I had to leave. The way the Army is treating soldiers with PTSD, TBI is beyond any type of betrayal I could possibly think of.

When soldiers are wounded with a physical wound, they treat them with respect; but soldiers with mental wounds are told their disability is because they were weak minded or a shamed or malingerer. I've been told all of that, and that I have a pre-existing condition. This whole thing has upset me to no end. Jen still says I should fight for what is right, but the way they're treating us is horrible, and quite frankly, dishonorable.

How can I fight again? I have to be a hero to those who are being treated like prisoners instead of heroes.

Today I was called a hero by a patient, and yet the Army does not recognize a disease that is clinically proven to be fact. It is also fact that the understanding of this disease is not getting to the front lines. No soldiers have to die in order for them to understand that all we want is acknowledgement for what we have been tortured in our minds with for so long. Just a little help in order to get back into the fight. If we can get better instead of being labeled cowards, then the Army would not have the force issues it has now. BETRAYAL!!

I do believe that a lot of my anxiety comes from a thing called survivor's guilt. This means that even though horrible things happened to me, more horrible things were shared, and I am alive to relive those episodes while others aren't.

It is difficult to place a face on where this guilt comes from, but I can associate the beginnings of my downhill run to Cash. Our trying to make it to him only to have him die was overwhelming to an 18-year-old kid. Since then, I told myself we will fight here again and never freeze in combat again. My whole career has been built on that last statement. To be a true warrior, you have to train your mind as well as your body.

I do believe that is why I was always first in combat, to live up to my promise to Cash, 17 years later. There has never been a mission I couldn't complete! I'm not talking about Army schools; I'm talking about real-life combat. Anyone can be book-smart, but do you have the ability to put it to use? That is why, regardless of what I wore on my left and right sleeve, men have always followed me, stood by me, and appreciated me for the type of combat leader I am. I firmly believe you can have all the bells and whistles on your chest, but that doesn't make you a teacher or a leader. A combat leader can be anyone who has the ability to step up when nobody else wants to; to have the ability to make sound, rational decisions when the chain is broken. This is the type of man, men follow – not his outward appearance, but a tough son of a bitch on the inside.

I believe the Army has it wrong. It should be men, mission, never leave a fallen comrade, never accept defeat, never quit, then men and women again. The battle is not won by awards or making a name for yourself in front of your superiors. It is won by smart fighting men and women who have the intestinal fortitude to see his soldiers come back from the patrol. It has always been that way. I remember when an officer asked me once for my opinion. I said, "Do you want the truth or a lie?" He said truth. I have always been able to tell the truth in this job. I don't sugar coat reality, and that is what America has to understand. The media sugar coats it. Rich men get rich while the poor man bleeds. Sometimes I even amaze myself with integrity for the corps, but I have never, ever had backs turn on us like what has happened in the whole system.

Part Two
Climbing Out

5 years later

It has been five years since I wrote those words. I think maybe some explanation are in order before we continue. I was just getting ready to be fired from being a Drill Instructor after 17 months on the trail. I was going through a Army investigation to prove my guilt. Because basically when you're wrong your wrong. However their might be some extenuating circumstances that help or hurt your case. So let's get real with each other right now.

I was under investigation for sexual harassment of a lower enlisted female. Career ending, I know. And that is exactly what happened to me. My carrier was over. However, what the Army, at the time did not understand was that, that was my escape. What? How can someone escape with sex? Well there are a lot of self medicating things you can do, I saw it every day by all the other battle buddies around me. Thiers booze, drugs, driving your car to fast, road rage, fighting, spouse abuse, child abuse, this list can go on and on. But you get my point. So I choose the one of the most dangerous reliefs there was sex. You ask, " why did I choose that?" I will explain later but let me just say it was a rush not to get caught, and isn't, that what combat vets need. That rush. A lot of my friends were using, but I was a Drill Instructor I didn't have time or the energy to use, or drink, there was just too much to do. So when I had the time I would jump on the computer. When you talk about war all day long, that is all you think about. I had so many flashbacks every day I sometimes forgot who I was. Looking into those young faces I could see the men that had lost their lives in Bagdad. It was just too much to handle. So I would turn to sex as my outlet. Anything was fine as long as it relieved my stress. Later in the book you will understand what stress is and I will give you some coping skills to deal with it.

So here I am five years later, retired and wondering what else could I have done differently to save my career, to relieve my stress, and to live healthier than I was before mentally. I lecture now and had a video made, plus, plus....... So what now. This next part is not going to be a self help moment in your life. I know you been looking for the answers to relieve your pain. I'm not going to give you a lists, and make you fill in about a hundred pages either. But what I am going to do is tell you how I made it. And yet still struggle with PTSD and TBI daily. I will however throw my lecture into the mix. Hey you followed me this far! So let's find the right thing to do together. So here is the first thing I want you to look at.

Tell your story

Now ,there are a lot of things you can do here.
The shrinks always want to make you write a journal.
That was the first part of my book, my darkness. The
words flew out of my pen like a bullet. Like I been
holding back all of that anger for so many years. Initially,
it just made things worse for me. It really set me back a
couple of years. I know getting it all on paper was just
the first step, and it was so painful it took me many
years to finish my thoughts. Any social worker worth
their salt will tell you that's the first step of many! I know
you tried, but writing it on paper doesn't solve your
problems; Your memories are still there, and they haunt
you with every page. It will help you begin to take
control of the memories that have been controlling you.
It will help, even if it doesn't seem like it at first. Trust in
the process.

I've also discovered sharing in a group
environment is really counterproductive. Because, admit
it, you are holding back for fear of rejection,
embarrassment, or the fact that you don't want your
weak side to come out. After all you're a soldier, and
soldiers don't cry. How can you overcome this problem?

Here is a possible solution.   Who is the one
person you really want to talk too? No fear of rejection
from the establishment.   No fear that if you break down
and cry that, that person will turn their back on you. No
fear that the person you trust won't leave you behind.
Who is that person? Think for a minute or two on this.
Soldiers do, with utter trust. No matter how bad the
situation is. Do you have that trust in someone? You
might be able to trust a buddy, a Chaplain, a social
worker, or even a complete stranger, but you have to do

this without holding anything back. I am always amazed that when I lecture someone always says, "Wow you didn't hold anything back." "That was amazing, how can you stand in front of so many soldiers and tell your story with such confidence?" The answer, my friends, is that I have learned to be honest with myself and trust who is listening to my lectures. There it is again, trust. Did you know that 60% of soldiers say they will not come forward because they don't trust the system enough to take care of them when they do come forward. That is a staggering stat, but a true one, as I found out.

When I was going through my investigation, Drill Instructors from all over Battalion would come up to me and say they wished they had the balls to finally get help, but they refused because it was career ending to go to mental health. In lies the stigma here, doesn't it? You can pretend to be "normal" and choose to be unhappy, get divorced, do drugs or booze, and any other negative coping skill, or you can swallow some pride and go get help. It is imperative you find people you can trust to take care of you. There is nothing good that comes from postponing treatment. You may think you are handling it. You may think no one notices a change in you. You may feel you have it all under control. If you have PTSD, you need help, this is not something to attempt to fix on your own. It is not worth the suffering. Get it fixed and get on with truly living.

Once you tell your story to someone that actually cares for you, you can start to heal. I mean let's be honest here, the Army is a corporation. It is a business which needs to operate, and not necessarily concerned with your well being and mental health. Some will take the view that it is easier to replace you than fix you. The nation's well being supersedes yours. These people in war have neither the time or energy to help you with your problems.   That is no excuse to stop you from getting help. The assistance is there, it is yours for the taking. Of all the courageous things you have done, none will be more important than admitting you need help and then letting nothing prevent you from getting it. Take a knee, the Army will be ready for you when you are healed. It can, and often, operates without you. Let it.

So, once again, who do you trust? I turned all my energy to telling my story to my wife of 18 years. I got all the bad shit off my chest, including all my computer stuff. I mean when you're facing charges you can't hide that. It was time to finally deal with everything. We cried together, we held each other, and we lost a lot of sleep. This was tricky at first because she was uneducated about PTSD and TBI, but she got on the computer and read everything she could find on the topics. Now, lord knows it doesn't excuse what I've done or the mistakes I will make in the future, and it wasn't an excuse, but she listened and trusted me and I trusted her. Once all that had been established, I wasn't a robot anymore. I was becoming human, and isn't that what we all want to be again after all those tours?

Maslow

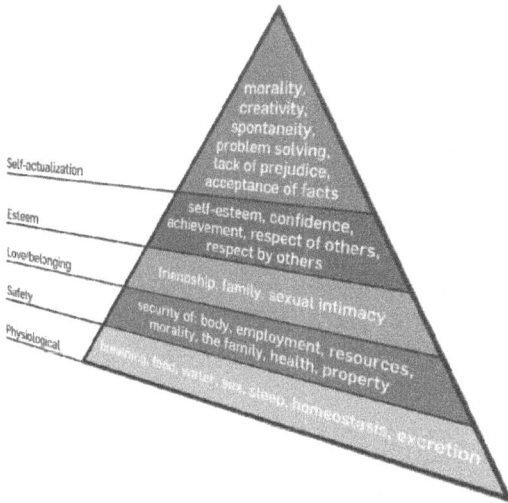

Maslow believed that all human emotion and feelings were tied to this chart, Hierarchy of Needs. This format is key to understanding where you are and how to fix the problem. Imagine this triangle as your base. The lord said you can't build a house on shifting sand. So let's take for example the sleep portion of the bottom of the pyramid. If you're not **sleeping** you can't rest. Walking a patrol around the perimeter of your house at night is not sleep. In this example, one block of the pyramid is missing in your life. If a block is missing or damaged, the pyramid will not stand. You cannot be a whole person if your pyramid is falling apart. Maslow felt we all need to complete one level and then move towards the next in able to be self-actualized. This is impossible with PTSD, you can see how many areas it can affect in your life.

I couldn't **sleep** for years, still can't really, but medication does help with that. However, stress plays a big part of sleep problems. Like I said if you're walking a perimeter at night, you are obviously stressed. I took a long hard look at what was stressing me and affecting my sleep .Once I figured that out I could begin to repair that block back of my pyramid.

The other parts of the bottom of the pyramid are what you receive when your deployed; **Food, water, and for some of you sex**. When any of those are missing, it leads to problems if not corrected. Let's move on to my biggest hurdle on the bottom of the pyramid.

SEX! For a lot of people this is an issue when they return. Most of us are lacking in this area when we are deployed. This need is not met, and needs to be fixed. Sex is an intimate act, and it can be difficult to express intimacy after returning from war. If you are depressed and separating yourself from everything around you, sex becomes even more difficult, and this need still goes unmet, and causing problems for you. This can also lead to more stress for you and your spouse. It seems like sex would be natural in a marriage, but war complicates many things, and sex is one of them. Not many are willing to discuss this subject, but I have a feeling there are staggering numbers of military families facing this problem.

For me, I tried to fill my sexual desires on the computer. That was an escape for me, and gave me feelings of pleasure that I had been missing. Pornography was not a solution to my problems, and only created more problems for me. It was against Army policy, but it was the only thing that made me feel human again.   Sex on tour was non-existent. When I was home with my wife, I was so far gone that I really wasn't in the mood or able to connect with her that way anymore. Why would she want to be with the monster I had become? Turning to something immoral, illegal by military standards, allowed me to feel that rush just like in combat, that I was missing. It is quite normal for warriors to want to find that rush after combat. Some will choose alcohol or drugs, driving fast, skydiving- I chose sex. It seemed safe. I thought I had it under control.

A lot of those emotions and feelings in this pyramid have to be addressed. It took me hitting the bottom to realize something was missing. I'm cannot sit here and you tell everything, most of it you have to figure out for yourself. Every person is different. Our experiences are different, we handle things differently, but it is hard to deny what pieces of your pyramid are falling apart. When that happens, it is time to get help.

Begin by moving up the pyramid. You have to fix the physiological needs first. Once you have a solid foundation, you are ready to work on the next step. The second level is hard to fulfill when you are deployed. **Safety**- always on guard, protecting you and your men. War zones are dangerous places. Even if you are not combat arms, there are dangers most people do not face. **Resources**- sometimes you're on your own to figure out the best solution in the field. It can be quite difficult to get every day items you need to survive. **Morality**- as you can tell from the first part of my book, morality isn't always black and white. There are always questions of morality and God in combat.   **Family**-Not very often is any part of your family with you in combat. Add to that the doubts about what your wife is home doing after the countless horror stories other soldiers are experiencing with their wives, wondering what your kids are doing and if you will be there to watch them grow up. When you are deployed you long to be home, but after deployment you just want to get back to where you know how to survive. You know what to do in combat, but it doesn't work in the "real world." What you need in the real world gets you killed in combat. You just can flip a switch and be ready to cope in whatever place you find yourself in. Soldiers like to think they can, but as hard as it is to admit, we are just human beings. See how tricky this crap is? There is no reason to ask why soldiers experience PTSD, the real question is how does combat not change who you are?

Consider this for a moment, when your return home you still pull guard, refuse to go to Wal-mart, and don't want to let anybody in your perimeter, even on the streets. Your whole tour you spend avoiding crowds and knowing at any moment any person can kill you or someone around you. It takes at least one to two years for a soldier to reacclimatize to the environment of being home. Most do not have that much time to adjust before they are once again planning to return to war. Everything is once again about fighting to stay alive, and postponing your transition to home. This is a blessing and a curse. PTSD behaviors help you survive in combat, but can cause you nothing but pain in the real world. I am often asked, "how do you get back into the swing of being home if you are slated to return in 9months.?" The true answer is- you don't. You stay combat ready in your mind and everything around you falls apart. You're ready to go back and you will. My case was I couldn't transition back to a normal mentality. I may have physically been in the United States, but everything I did or saw had me in Iraq. I wasn't just training Privates, I was preparing them to fight and I knew some of them would die. Not many of my trainees were combat arms, but in my mind, they were all going to be fighting the same enemy I had been fighting, and was still fighting. I knew going back was inevitable, I let myself believe I was staying sharp- like the tip of the sword should. I had work left to do, I had brothers whose deaths I wanted revenge for, everything was about returning back to kill the enemy. I was not home. I wouldn't let myself be. I couldn't. To those around me, I was falling apart. People could see this, I could not. I was fighting a different battle and didn't even know.

For many years I blamed myself on decisions that weren't mine to make. You can't control when some jerk is in the head shed looking at that the battle through a lens and makes a decision that effects you on the ground. There are days when those bad decisions result in the loss of a fellow soldier. An internal conflict begins because you know you should follow orders, but you also need to bring your men home alive. This scenario is played out daily on the battlefield. Soon you become numb to it, and just do it. Seeing fallen comrades numbs your heart, but you don't have time to mourn in combat. That will wait for another day. Delaying the normal grief process does not make it any easier. It just compounds the issues you have to deal with when you return home. Your nights are spent reliving the deaths and wondering if you are responsible even though you did not pull the trigger. Before you know it, you wonder if killing the enemy is even moral. Yes, it is the job you swore to do, but was it really necessary to take the lives you did? This forces you to questions your morality down to your soul. Are you a soldier or a monster? When you question yourself in this way, it blurs all your emotions. Love, hate, stress, warmth, are all the same. Those emotions that kept you alive in combat are not necessarily the emotions you want to put bring home with you. It is a challenge to figure out how to deal with your traumatic experiences and adjust to normal life. **You have to let go! Some things just happen and you can't wrap your head around them. Let it go, brother, or take everything around you down with the ship.**

When you notice your life is crumbling around you, you try to fill it with anything and everything that will bring you peace. Sometimes we solve the problems quickly, easily, and appropriately. Sometimes, you can't seem to get free of the pain. Your actions can now start affecting the third level of the pyramid. Once others are noticing, it is even more difficult for you to overcome this on your own. This is the place where it is easier to push more people out of your life, then it is to deal with your issues. These people are probably the people who will be there to help you on your journey to recovery. You can't have a complete pyramid without them, and you can't get to the next level alone. It is still the goal of all of us to reach the top of the pyramid. I tried to get through without anyone, and I can say it was a complete failure.

With every part of you crumbling, it isn't hard to imagine your esteem will take a hit. Not just how you view yourself, but what feedback you are getting from others. If you aren't feeling your best, you will not be putting forth your best effort. Your job performance will likely slip, and most bosses have no problems pointing this out to you. It is not what you need to hear at the time, you feel bad enough. Sometimes pyramids crumble from the bottom, but this level is a place quite common for cracks to begin. You may question whether other people respected your work in combat or understand that you did what you had to do. You may not even be happy about your drop in performance, but you also just may not care. Your self esteem dwindles to nothing and deep depression sets in. All of this can be related to the increasing number of suicides in the Army since combat operations began in Iraq and Afghanistan. This level can cause a vicious cycle of guilt that is hard to break away from.

Now once all of this shit in your head is straight you might be able to reach the top of the pyramid. Let's be honest here, it can take a "normal" person a lifetime to reach the top. It is a continual process, make sure you are constantly building and rebuilding. Aim for the top in all that you do. Make sure you always have a strong foundation. It is important to take care of yourself so that you are able to positively impact others. Post Traumatic Stress complicates your life for a while, but it can be overcome. You can rebuild, no matter how much damage is done. Start with one brick at a time, and before you know it you will have constructed something amazing.

Conclusion and Thanks

I wanted to take a moment in the ending of this book to say thank you to all my personal friends that stuck with me through my darkest hours.   I watched many walk away, but will be eternally grateful for those who gave me a hand up when I needed it the most.

I wanted to say thank you to my wife of 20 years, Jennifer. You truly are the rock of this relationship.

I also want to thank my boys. I brought war into the house and you saw firsthand the devastating effects of it. Thank you for being you and understanding.   You are definitely the best thing I have ever done, or ever will do.

And last, I want to say thanks to the men who fought so hard to make things right in a country that didn't want us there. We changed the world, and I hope it hasn't changed you.

To all of you that have been battling this for so many years, I sincerely hope you will find peace, and I hope that this book can relate to you somehow. Don't let PTSD take anything from you, it is a battle you can win!

Let it go!

The following information was presented by the National Center on PTSD and is very usefull

A HELPING HAND SHEET
FOR SOMEONE IN NEED

Helping a family member who has PTSD

When someone has PTSD can change family life. The person with PTSD may act differently and get angry easily. He or she may not want to do things you used to enjoy together.

You may feel scared and frustrated about the changes you see in your loved one. You also may feel angry about what's happening to your family, or wonder if things will ever go back to the way they were. These feelings and worries are common in people who have a family member with PTSD.

It is important to learn about PTSD so you can understand why it happened, how it is treated, and what you can do to help. But you also need to take care of yourself. Changes in family life are stressful, and taking care of yourself will make it easier to cope.

How can I help?

You may feel helpless, but there are many things you can do. Nobody expects you to have all the answers.

Here are ways you can help:

- Learn as much as you can about PTSD. Knowing how PTSD affects people may help you understand what your family member is going through. The more you know, the better you and your family can handle PTSD.

- Offer to go to doctor visits with your family member. You can help keep track of medicine and therapy, and you can be there for support.
- Tell your loved one you want to listen and that you also understand if he or she doesn't feel like talking.
- Plan family activities together, like having dinner or going to a movie.
- Take a walk, go for a bike ride, or do some other physical activity together. Exercise is important for health and helps clear your mind.
- Encourage contact with family and close friends. A support system will help your family member get through difficult changes and stressful times.

Your family member may not want your help. If this happens, keep in mind that withdrawal can be a symptom of PTSD. A person who withdraws may not feel like talking, taking part in group activities, or being around other people. Give your loved one space, but tell him or her that you will always be ready to help.

How can I deal with anger or violent behavior?

Your family member may feel angry about many things. Anger is a normal reaction to trauma, but it can hurt relationships and make it hard to think clearly. Anger also can be frightening.

If anger leads to violent behavior or abuse, it's dangerous. Go to a safe place and call for help right away. Make sure children are in a safe place as well.

It's hard to talk to someone who is angry. One thing you can do is set up a time-out system. This helps you find a way to talk even while angry. Here's one way to do this.

- Agree that either of you can call a time-out at any time.
- Agree that when someone calls a time-out, the discussion must stop right then.
- Decide on a signal you will use to call a time-out. The signal can be a word that you say or a hand signal.
- Agree to tell each other where you will be and what you will be doing during the time-out. Tell each other what time you will come back.

While you are taking a time-out, don't focus on how angry you feel. Instead, think calmly about how you will talk things over and solve the problem.

After you come back:

- Take turns talking about solutions to the problem. Listen without interrupting.
- Use statements starting with "I," such as "I think" or "I feel." Using "you" statements can sound accusing.
- Be open to each other's ideas. Don't criticize each other.
- Focus on things you both think will work. It's likely you will both have good ideas.
- Together, agree which solutions you will use.

How can I communicate better?

You and your family may have trouble talking about feelings, worries, and everyday problems. Here are some ways to communicate better:

- Be clear and to the point.
- Be positive. Blame and negative talk won't help the situation.
- Be a good listener. Don't argue or interrupt. Repeat what you hear to make sure you understand, and ask questions if you need to know more.
- Put your feelings into words. Your loved one may not know you are sad or frustrated unless you are clear about your feelings.
- Help your family member put feelings into words. Ask, "Are you feeling angry? Sad? Worried?"
- Ask how you can help.
- Don't give advice unless you are asked.

if your family is having a lot of trouble talking things over, consider trying family therapy. Family therapy is a type of counseling that involves your whole family. A therapist helps you and your family communicate, maintain good relationships, and cope with tough emotions.

During therapy, each person can talk about how a problem is affecting the family. Family therapy can help family members understand and cope with PTSD.

Your health professional or a religious or social services organization can help you find a family therapist who specializes in PTSD.

How can I take care of myself?

Helping a person with PTSD can be hard on you. You may have your own feelings of fear and anger about the trauma. You may feel guilty because you wish your family member would just forget his or her problems and get on with life. You may feel confused or frustrated because your loved one has changed, and you may worry that your family life will never get back to normal.

All of this can drain you. It can affect your health and make it hard for you to help your loved one. If you're not careful, you may get sick yourself, become depressed, or burn out and stop helping your loved one.

To help yourself, you need to take care of yourself and have other people help you.

Care for yourself

- Don't feel guilty or feel that you have to know it all. Remind yourself that nobody has all the answers. It's normal to feel helpless at times.
- Don't feel bad if things change slowly. You cannot change anyone. People have to change themselves.
- Take care of your physical and mental health. If you feel yourself getting sick or often feel sad and hopeless, see your doctor.
- Don't give up your outside life. Make time for activities and hobbies you enjoy. Continue to see your friends.
- Take time to be by yourself. Find a quiet place to gather your thoughts and "recharge."
- Get regular exercise, even just a few minutes a day. Exercise is a healthy way to deal with stress.
- Eat healthy foods. When you are busy, it may seem easier to eat fast food than to prepare healthy meals. But healthy foods will give you

more energy to carry you through the day.
- Remember the good things. It's easy to get weighed down by worry and stress. But don't forget to see and celebrate the good things that happen to you and your family.

Get help

During difficult times, it is important to have people in your life who you can depend on. These people are your support network. They can help you with everyday jobs, like taking a child to school, or by giving you love and understanding.

You may get support from:

- Family members.
- Friends, coworkers, and neighbors.
- Members of your religious or spiritual group.
- Support groups.
- Doctors and other health professionals

The main features of PTSD can be summarized as follows: **How is PTSD Measured?**

How can one tell if distress after a personal tragedy is a normal reaction to an upsetting life experience or something more serious?

It can be difficult to know whether distress is a normal reaction or a symptom of something more serious. Even experts may require the results of a detailed evaluation to answer this question. Posttraumatic Stress Disorder (PTSD) is only one of many possible reactions to a traumatic experience. After a trauma, some people become anxious, some become depressed, and many find that they are not able to deal with their responsibilities as well as they had before the trauma. Although the majority of people are distressed for a while, over a period of a few weeks to a few months, most find that their upset lessens and they are better able to function. Someone who continues to be profoundly affected by their experience several months or even years later may be struggling with PTSD.

What is PTSD?

The main features of PTSD can be summarized as follows:

Trauma

PTSD is different from most mental-health diagnoses because it is tied to a to particular life experience. A traumatic experience typically involves the potential for death or serious injury resulting in intense fear, helplessness, or horror.

Symptoms

PTSD is characterized by a specific group of symptoms that sets it apart from other types of reactions to trauma. Increasingly, evidence points to four major types of symptoms: re-experiencing, avoidance, numbing, and arousal.

Re-experiencing symptoms

These symptoms involve a sort of mental replay of the trauma, often accompanied by strong emotional reactions. This can happen in reaction to thoughts or reminders of the experience when the person is awake or in the form of nightmares during sleep.

Avoidance symptoms

Are often exhibited as efforts to evade activities, places, or people that are reminders of the trauma.

Numbing symptoms

These are typically experienced as a loss of emotions, particularly positive feelings.

Arousal symptoms

Arousal symptoms reflect excessive physiological activation and include a heightened sense of being on guard as well as difficulty with sleep and concentration.

Length and Severity

To qualify for a formal diagnosis, the symptoms must persist for over one month, cause significant distress, and affect the individual's ability to function socially, occupationally, or domestically.

How do I get an evaluation?

While it may be tempting to identify PTSD for yourself or someone you know, the diagnosis generally is made by a mental-health professional. This will usually involve a formal evaluation by a psychiatrist, psychologist, or clinical social worker who is specifically trained to assess psychological problems.

What can I expect from an evaluation for PTSD?

The nature of an evaluation for PTSD can vary widely depending on how the evaluation will be used and the training of the professional evaluator. An interviewer may take as little as 15 minutes to get a sense of your traumatic experience and the effect it has had on your life in order to determine whether treatment for PTSD is called for. On the other hand, a specialized PTSD assessment can take eight or more 1-hour sessions when the information is needed for legal or disability claims. Regardless of the length of the evaluation, you can expect to be questioned in depth about experiences that may have been traumatic for you and about symptoms you may be experiencing as a result of these experiences. Evaluations that are more thorough are likely to involve detailed, structured interviews and psychological tests on which you record your thoughts and feeling. Your spouse or partner may be asked to provide additional information, and you may undergo a procedure that examines your physiological reactions to mild reminders of your trauma. Whatever the particulars of your situation, you should always be able to find out in advance from the professional conducting the evaluation what the assessment will involve and what information it is expected to provide.

What are some of the common assessments for PTSD?

As noted above, two main categories of PTSD evaluations are structured interviews and self-report questionnaires. The Clinician Administered PTSD Scale (CAPS) was developed by National Center for PTSD staff and is among the most widely used types of interviews. It has a format that requests information about the frequency and intensity of the core PTSD symptoms and of some common associated symptoms, which may have important implications for treatment and recovery. Another widely used interview is the Structured Clinical Interview for DSM (SCID). The SCID can be used to assess a range of psychiatric disorders including PTSD. Other interview instruments include the Anxiety Disorders Interview Schedule-Revised (ADIS), the PTSD-Interview, the Structured Interview for PTSD (SI-PTSD), and the PTSD Symptom Scale Interview (PSS-I). Each has unique features that might make it a good choice for a particular evaluation.

Several self-report measures have also been developed as time- and cost-efficient vehicles for obtaining information about PTSD-related distress. These measures provide a single score representing the amount of distress an individual is experiencing. Among this set is another widely used measure developed by National Center for PTSD staff, the PTSD Checklist (PCL). This measure comes in two versions, one oriented for civilians and another specifically designed for military personnel and veterans. Other widely used self-report measures are the Impact of Event Scale-Revised (IES-R), the Keane PTSD Scale of the MMPI-2, the Mississippi Scale for Combat Related PTSD and the Mississippi Scale for Civilians, the Posttraumatic Diagnostic Scale (PDS), the Penn Inventory for Posttraumatic Stress, and the Los Angeles Symptom Checklist (LASC).

National center PTSD, USA